Praise for *Infinite Receiving*®

'Suzy asks brilliant questions, whic[h]
your inner beliefs with your action[s]
a life of ease and abundance. [A]

SUZY WALKER, METR[O]

'Through her proven methods and her own commitment to the
embodiment of her work, Suzy Ashworth shows you how you
can truly have it all. Get ready to upgrade your operating system
and unlock new levels of fun, freedom, and flow using the tools
within this book. Just like Suzy, *Infinite Receiving* is a vibe!'

NIYC PIDGEON, POSITIVE PSYCHOLOGIST, BUSINESS MENTOR,
AND AUTHOR OF *NOW IS YOUR CHANCE*

'This book unlocks your unlimited potential to have anything
you want! I loved the practical strategies on how to expand
wealth consciousness. Suzy reminds you that you are safe and
worthy of co-creating miracles beyond your wildest dreams.'

JADAH SELLNER, AUTHOR OF *SHE BUILDS* AND *SIMPLE GREEN
SMOOTHIES*, AND HOST OF THE *LEAD WITH LOVE* PODCAST

'When I got the news that Suzy Ashworth was finally writing
this book, I was so excited for the world! Suzy is the epitome of
authenticity and just by being in her presence, I feel infinitely
worthy. This book is a must for anyone who's ready to live
a full and whole life filled with prosperity in all forms.'

KYLE GRAY, BEST-SELLING AUTHOR OF *RAISE YOUR VIBRATION* AND
ANGEL NUMBERS

'Suzy Ashworth is an absolute force when it comes to
calibrating to new levels of wealth, freedom, and abundance
across all areas of life. She's changed my life and I can't wait
for this book to change yours. Start reading if you are ready
and willing to quantum leap beyond your wildest dreams!'

MEL WELLS, BEST-SELLING AUTHOR OF
THE GODDESS REVOLUTION AND *HUNGRY FOR MORE*

'How infinite can you become when it comes to receiving? You are about to find out. Suzy takes you on a journey to help you [make] one-degree-a-day change to create your next level of abundance and receptivity…. Now, we are all lucky enough to receive Suzy's brilliant coaching.'

EMILY FLETCHER, FOUNDER OF ZIVA MEDITATION AND BEST-SELLING AUTHOR OF *STRESS LESS, ACCOMPLISH MORE*

'What a refreshing, original book to guide us all into greater levels of wealth, material, and otherwise. I found myself nodding along with every chapter and being invited to deepen my connection to and understanding of receiving on every level. I highly recommend this book to anyone who's longing for expansion.'

KATE NORTHRUP, BEST-SELLING AUTHOR OF *DO LESS* AND *MONEY: A LOVE STORY*

'This book is a phenomenal gift to the world and anyone looking to take their life to the next level.'

KOYA WEBB, LIFE COACH, SPEAKER, AND AUTHOR OF *LET YOUR FEARS MAKE YOU FIERCE*

'I love Suzy and her book *Infinite Receiving!* It's a manifestation book with a difference. A must-read for anyone wanting to tap into their unlimited potential and consciously co-create with the abundance of the universe, while keeping it real and not just acquiring more 'stuff.' It'll help you create a life that is deeply aligned to your soul and beyond your wildest dreams.'

REBECCA CAMPBELL, BEST-SELLING AUTHOR OF *RISE SISTER RISE*

'Suzy is a spiritual woman who stands for and with all women; a girl's girl and woman's woman who wants us all to succeed and have the courage of our convictions. Not only does she walk the walk and talk the talk, she truly believes and lives by these principles and standards…. Whatever you are trying to achieve, even if you are doing it alone, this book is like having the most confident and reassuring partner by your side helping you to make it all come together.'

SINITTA, SINGER AND ENTERTAINER

Infinite
Receiving®

Infinite Receiving®

Crack the code to conscious
wealth creation and finally
manifest your dream life

SUZY ASHWORTH

HAY HOUSE
Carlsbad, California • New York City
London • Sydney • New Delhi

Published in the United Kingdom by:
Hay House UK Ltd, The Sixth Floor, Watson House,
54 Baker Street, London W1U 7BU
Tel: +44 (0)20 3927 7290; Fax: +44 (0)20 3927 7291; www.hayhouse.co.uk

Published in the United States of America by:
Hay House Inc., PO Box 5100, Carlsbad, CA 92018-5100
Tel: (1) 760 431 7695 or (800) 654 5126
Fax: (1) 760 431 6948 or (800) 650 5115; www.hayhouse.com

Published in Australia by:
Hay House Australia Pty Ltd, 18/36 Ralph St, Alexandria NSW 2015
Tel: (61) 2 9669 4299; Fax: (61) 2 9669 4144; www.hayhouse.com.au

Published in India by:
Hay House Publishers India, Muskaan Complex,
Plot No.3, B-2, Vasant Kunj, New Delhi 110 070
Tel: (91) 11 4176 1620; Fax: (91) 11 4176 1630; www.hayhouse.co.in

A catalogue record for this book is available from the British Library.

Tradepaper ISBN: 978-1-4019-7487-9
E-book ISBN: 978-1-83782-043-6
Audiobook ISBN: 978-1-83782-042-9

Interior illustrations: 6, 34, 62, 91, 92, 93: © Suzy Ashworth; all other illustrations: Shutterstock

10 9 8 7 6 5 4 3 2 1

Printed in the United States of America

This product uses papers sourced from responsibly managed forests. For more information, see www.hayhouse.com.

To Caesar, Coco, and Aluna,
May you know what it means to live from a frequency
of Infinite Receiving in every cell of your beings as you
forge your own paths in this world.
Love, Mum x

Contents

Foreword

I was speaking at a conference and the organizer said, "Last year's guest was the best keynote speaker I've ever seen. Everyone said so."

Well, no pressure then!

Who was this incredible person? Suzy Ashworth!

Here's the thing. Suzy really is magical. Everyone who comes into contact with Suzy in any way comes away changed forever. She's that powerful, and she makes you feel that way, too.

Suzy inspires you to elevate every part of your life. I even started dreaming of the outfits we'd wear if/when we shared a stage together. She makes you believe you can pull off a catsuit and thigh-high boots!

We live in a time of infinite abundance and possibility. We have the opportunities and technology to make all of our dreams come true. But…

We also live in a world where things feel scary and uncertain. And most people have a lot of guilt about building wealth. I get it.

Making money isn't hard. Just sell something to someone who needs it. Repeat. I've made tens of millions of dollars doing that.

But true abundance isn't about transactions. Most of us want the world to be a better place, not just to make money to get more stuff.

Infinite Receiving will help you build wealth inside and out. So, it doesn't matter what new technology comes out; you'll have that inner knowing that you'll always be okay. That you deserve everything you desire.

We all have a lot of baggage about what we're allowed to be, do, and have. Work your way through the chapters and release your fears.

This is the necessary inner work. You can create anything, but you have to work through your resistance. It's okay to be afraid. We all are, even me and Suzy, even though we're fancy published authors!

Suzy inspires me endlessly to be more adventurous as a businesswoman, a mother, and a creator. And I know she'll inspire you, too.

I hope you get to experience Suzy in person one day. Until then, this book is the next best thing. When you're done, get in her world in any way you can.

You don't have to do this alone,

Denise Duffield-Thomas

Author of *Chill and Prosper*

Introduction

When I sat down to write this book, I asked myself a question that's probably slightly different from the question many writers in my genre might ask. Instead of 'Who am I writing for?' I began with *why*. Why would anyone want to pick up this book? Why would someone be intrigued by the idea of Infinite Receiving (IR), and what it can offer them?

When I pictured you, dear reader, reading this, I saw – or more accurately, I sensed – someone who already knows deep down that there's so much more out there for them. What I felt was hope. A sense of unlimited potential, the energy of possibility and the excitement that comes with it. I felt your willingness to ask yourself, 'What if...?' To wonder, 'What if it's not just that anything is possible... but what if anything is possible for *me*?'

I also sensed your doubts and perhaps even a little tinge of disappointment around your past efforts and the times when it seemed like your attempts to improve your life, career, or business fell short. Perhaps you've found yourself wondering, 'When will enough be enough? Shouldn't I be happy with what I already have?' It's natural to wonder why so many rich, famous individuals who appear to have it all still seem unhappy and unfulfilled. And to question how it's possible to be satisfied with what we have, when we're always in pursuit of what's next.

If any of this sounds familiar, you're in the right place. Here's the thing: *Infinite Receiving* isn't just another manifestation book telling you the secret to how you can have it all – although, if that's what you want, it's all yours, baby!

Infinite Receiving – the lowdown

So, what's *Infinite Receiving* all about? And, more importantly, how is it different from every other book you've read on manifesting the life of your dreams?

Infinite Receiving is a lifestyle and a philosophy – but more than that, it's a *frequency*. If that sounds strange – don't worry; I'll explain what I mean by that in the coming chapters. For now, consider Infinite Receiving simply as a way of looking at and interacting with the world that makes getting precisely what you need in a given moment not just possible, but inevitable. And, as you become more familiar with looking at life from this unique viewpoint, I'm going to show you how to move beyond getting what you need, to accessing exactly what you desire. Because, yes, you *can* have both!

I call this **conscious co-creating** because it's you, flowing and operating in tandem with the abundance available to us all within the universe. And as you stretch your Infinite Receiving muscle, you'll notice that it's easier to enjoy the experience of receiving more of what you actually want, whether that's more love, more joy, more peace, more money, more business opportunities – you get to choose. Now comes the best part: Everyone's idea of 'more' is unique, and that's what really gets me excited!

Why? Because people have been selling the secrets of 'getting what you want' for millennia, but the truth is, getting what you want is the easy bit. What's way more challenging is avoiding the *feeling* of anticlimax when you finally get the contract you were chasing, the car you have always wanted. Or the house, the promotion, or dare I say it, the partner. Because it doesn't make you feel better. Well, not for long anyway.

I mean, can you imagine living in a world where people *didn't* need to get more stuff to feel more worthy, more valuable, or deserving? A world where you didn't work all the hours of the day to get the thing that was supposed to make you the envy of your neighbors but, in reality, left you feeling hollow and inferior? And let's not forget those so-called 'lucky' lottery and competition winners. The ones who thought they'd hit the jackpot or won the prize of a lifetime, only to realize how fleeting the momentary high is, and how quickly it leaves them craving more. Sounds like addiction, right? Yep – because it is.

I completely understand why so many people decide that the way forward is the simple life. Renouncing money and deciding that if they don't need it, then they shouldn't have it, because more doesn't make you happy. I get it, I really do.

While studies have shown a correlation between increased earnings and well-being, we also know that it doesn't follow that more money equals more happiness. But, like it or not, money is useful – it increases the choices available to us in our modern world, from where and how we live, to the quality of our healthcare, and more.

Infinite Receiving, however, isn't just about the money. Or about getting more for more's sake.

Simply stated, it's about human potential. It's about knowing with every cell in your body that, no matter where you are in your life circumstances right now, no matter how good or bad things are around you, your potential to create is limitless. It always has been and always will be. You were born with the ability to be a conscious co-creator, and when you fully understand this, step into your power, and embrace this path, it changes the game! From this place, you're not living to score points or prove your worth. Instead, you're making the conscious choice to recognize that the boundless potential housed within your body is what makes you extraordinary – it makes you magic.

And when I say 'magic,' I also mean worthy and deserving, and 'enough' just because you're you. From that place, you play the game of co-creation because you can, because it's fun. And if you feel called to do so, you get to use your magic in your own unique way to help others discover their own limitless potential, too.

I describe conscious co-creating from this state of being as creating from a place of abundance, or fullness.

In the coming pages, I'll be sharing with you exactly what it means to know your fullness, which puts you in the optimum place for consciously co-creating all your desires, simply because it's fun, because you can, because that's what limitless co-creators do!

And it's from this perspective that, if a 'creation apocalypse' happened tomorrow and you were told you could never make or create another thing in your life again, you wouldn't feel lost or in doubt about who you are because you're not creating to show off or prove something to the outside world. You'd still know your worth and value and the magic of who you are just by being yourself. I know – wild concept, right?

This is a world where you still feel full and complete as a human because fullness is your *starting* point. And everything else that you do, achieve, or acquire is a bonus that sits on top of your fullness – your *completeness*. It's the cherry on top of a cake that doesn't detract from the deliciousness of the cake if it's taken away. It's wild and beautiful and it is my deep desire for you to know this feeling for yourself.

When you decide to say 'yes' to operating through this lens, your life will change. And I'm not going to lie – this is a big decision. This road won't always feel like it is the simplest one, so hold fire on your commitment until I ask you if you're really ready to go all in. But when you do make the decision to commit, something amazing happens. After the initial excitement of embracing something new wears off, many people find themselves experiencing a deep sense of inner calm. They start to embrace their past, accept the present, and eagerly anticipate what's up ahead. And let me tell you, there's something magical about this stage as they ready themselves for the incredible things about to come their way.

I encourage you to tap into this feeling, too. From this place of fullness, you can both give yourself permission to ask for what you want and become the person who's ready to receive those desires. Fun, play, and adventure can be at the top of your calendar and to-do list if you desire them, along with the space to allow guilt-free time away from 'responsibilities' to renew, reset, restore, and recharge.

Or perhaps now is your time to focus on that project you have been putting off, because you haven't felt 'good enough' to even start. Maybe you're worried about what might happen if you actually succeed. This fear is more common than you think, and when it's at play, it becomes easier to prioritize everyone else's needs and wants above your own. Feeling tired at the end of the day or just not having enough time may have seemed like good reasons not to put your best foot forward – until now.

With Infinite Receiving, you get to let go of these fears. You get to live your life knowing that you are enough, just as you are, with all your imperfections. You come to understand that anything you do from an 'achievement' or 'challenge' perspective doesn't make you a better or more worthy person. That those things are like fringe benefits – not necessary to make life more fulfilling. They don't change who you are at your core.

Abundant living

This is a wildly abundant way to live your life. When you live your life from a place of fullness, abundance is the natural outcome. Your life can't help but feel rich and overflowing. And yes, this counts even in the most challenging of contexts – in fact, *especially* in those times and situations.

And then there's the money aspect. In my experience of working in close proximity to hundreds of entrepreneurs and clients, I've observed that financial abundance drops in at different times for different people. Sometimes it happens quickly and other times, it takes longer. I invite you to trust the timeline and the process. As you stay committed to the journey, you'll naturally elevate your relationship with money and become more receptive to abundance.

And that gets to be really fun!

Level up

Here's a question for you: 'What does your *next level* of financial freedom look like?' Notice I said 'next level,' rather than 'ultimate vision.' This isn't because I don't believe that your ultimate dream is possible; it's because for most people their relationship with money is so entangled with their own self-worth that, while dreaming about lottery-proportioned windfalls sounds fun and exciting, it rarely helps a person take the small steps required, practically and emotionally, to break the patterns they have built up over a lifetime.

So, what would the next level mean for you? It might mean you get to buy back some of your time by hiring support in your business or around your home. More freedom to choose the house or the holiday that you actually desire, rather than going for second best because that feels more 'logical' or 'sensible.' Perhaps for you it will mean being able to donate more to your favorite causes and charities. Or treating your friends and family without the worry that one day you're going to feel resentful or taken advantage of.

Whatever it means for you, when you choose Infinite Receiving, you are effectively choosing yourself. But rather than that being a selfish thing, the ripple effect you get to have on the people and communities that are important to you can be felt long after your initial intention and excitement have faded. Once you're consciously choosing to live in 'receiving mode,' your energy is at its most potent. It's when you are most truly attractive – inside and out. As you live from that state of deep appreciation for all that you are and all that you are receiving on a daily basis, people begin to look and interact with you differently. It's wild. You'll walk into a shop and the shop assistant will have to ask you what you do, because there's just 'something about you.' Or you'll be at an event and even though you're not more dressed up than usual, people and smiles will find their way to you like moths to a flame. Because people can feel your magnetism.

In my work, I'm lucky to meet people from different walks of life from all over the world. One thing I feel most privileged to receive happens when people come up to me and tell me how I make them feel. They say things like: 'I feel so energized after speaking with you,' or 'I don't know why, but our conversation has given me hope and a new sense of purpose.' Infinite Receiving is the frequency that makes people say those things. It reminds me of Maya Angelou's wisdom: 'People may forget what you said, people may forget what you did, but they will never forget how you made them feel.' Because when others feel better simply by being in your presence, you can be sure that Infinite Receiving is at work!

But Infinite Receiving isn't all unicorns and rainbows. It's real. When we're in receiving mode, we're looking at more abundance, more love, more trust – and more resilience. And the resilience piece of the work that we do is really, really big, because being an Infinite Receiver doesn't mean you get to escape challenge. The difference is, when you choose this path, you will have a whole new set of tools to deal with difficult people, situations, and experiences way more effectively than you have ever done before.

What I know to be true is this: It is totally possible to create a 'pinch me' life. A life where you look around at your friends, your family, the work that you do and want to squeal with joy at the life you have created. I know that it's possible to defy the odds and surpass the expectations of the group or labels other people may have given you, or perhaps you have even given yourself before you were ready to know that something else was available to you.

How do I know that for sure? Because I, Suzy Ashworth, have done it. Yep – I, a single mum of three glorious children, product of the late-seventies' foster-care system, whose formal education stopped for over 15 years after I graduated from high school at 16 (not because I was supposed to finish there, but because I dropped out of college), am living proof that we can write a different story for ourselves if we choose to. We get to receive more than we ever thought was possible.

Consider this book as your trusty manual and guide to the *how* of manifesting your business and life dreams with clarity and confidence. So, where do you start? You start with more. And by getting very specific about what 'more' looks like, feels like, and even tastes like for you. And you'll have a chance to do this using the Wheel of Infinite Receiving exercise on p.6.

So that's the what; let's talk about the how...

In Part I, we're going to start reimagining and/or upgrading the way we look at wealth. And then, in Part II, we'll talk about how you can create more of it in your life through a framework that I call the Four Pillars – these are the tools you'll use to grow your business and expand your wealth professionally and personally.

The process is non-linear. Even if you apply just one of these Pillars, you will change your life. And the work doesn't stop when you finish reading this book. What I share here is a lifelong journey and I, too, am still a student of the teachings. While everything I've written in this book comes from my direct experience, everything I write is also a learning experience for me, and an opportunity to remind myself of how I get to continue to deepen this practice of Infinite Receiving.

You don't need to read the book from front to back for everything to make sense. I still recommend, however, that for your first time reading, you do exactly that. Then, once you have completed it, either go back to the beginning of the book or see what page the book falls open on and trust intuitively that this is your opportunity to deepen your own practice today.

What I can tell you for sure is that while one Pillar on its own has magic so potent it can change the trajectory of your life, when you put all four Pillars together, the magic that's possible is mind-blowing. The Pillars are:

- the Pillar of Infinite Greatness

- the Pillar of Infinite Support

- the Pillar of Infinite Love

- the Pillar of Infinite Conscious Creation

Together, they make up the framework for creating a life where you are consciously and infinitely receiving.

I'm excited because in every chapter, you'll find practical ways to implement the theory in the form of exercises, meditations, and affirmations. I love to dance, and I use music and dance in my talks and coaching sessions. I've included a playlist of my favorite tracks on p.235. If music is your thing, you can play any of the tracks that feel appropriate before or after reading a chapter.

Everything I share here is the work that I do. It's simple and potent, but it's not always easy. So, do yourself a favor and commit to playing the game alongside me for at least 30 days, and commit to noticing the differences in how you feel, how you view life and, of course, what you are receiving.

Throughout the book, I'll also be answering some of the most common questions that my clients in the Infinite Receiving program ask me in relation to each of the Pillars. And you'll find additional support and teachings on my website and in the Infinite Receiving community that already exists online – see p.235.

If you want the Infinite Receiving method to truly take hold, I encourage you to go through the pages of this book multiple times. Every time you read and reread the book, the message is going to resonate more and more deeply with you. This isn't a 'one and done' book. And as you see the magic unfold in your own life, my hope is that you'll share this book with other people in your life. Maybe you'll even want to complete the Infinite Receiving Coaching Certification and empower others to experience this transformative practice for themselves. Either way, while I hope that at the end of the book you'll be saying things like, 'Oh my god, these incredible changes are happening,' what I know for sure is that this is foundational work for life. It's not just a temporary fix. It's. For. Life.

Even so, after we've gone over the fundamentals of Infinite Receiving and unpacked the feelings that come up for you, and you've fully grasped what it's all about, don't be surprised if you find yourself having moments when doubts creep back in. That's natural.

There will be times when you forget…. Times when you feel like you're on your own…. Times when you feel like the responsibility of 'getting everything right' is all on your shoulders.

What's important is learning how to return to and sustain the *feeling* of being your unique, astonishing self, and the knowing that this Infinite Receiving method gives you.

Remember, when you stumble and fall off track (as we all inevitably do), the key to success lies in how many times you choose to pick yourself back up. It's about how quickly you can realign with the frequency of your most expansive self. Then the moments of doubt will become briefer, and the periods of embracing your remarkable self will continue to expand and flourish.

Getting started

For those of you who are new to this type of work, my invitation for you is to suspend any disbelief for the time we spend together in these pages – depending on how quickly you like to read, that's probably around 30 days. For just 30 days, you get to ask yourself, 'What if? What if this could be true *for me?*'

Let's journey together as I share what I've learned and what has worked for me. From the things that I genuinely feel I've mastered to the things that I still tussle with, but that have already made a difference in my life.

My commitment to myself and to this life is to be a 'forever student.'

The only thing I can promise you is that I'm not perfect and I definitely don't have it all figured out. But to wait until I've reached 'perfection' before I share the lessons and the magic that are already happening for me just wasn't an option. So – from this position of eager and excited student – here we are.

Now, at the same time as asking you to suspend disbelief, I'm also going to ask you not to abandon yourself. If something feels really jarring, take what works for you and leave what doesn't. But while I invite you to leave what doesn't vibe with you, I'd like you to ask yourself this: 'If this principle is about helping me to achieve, do, or see X, what would I need to shift, release, or choose to see differently in my current thinking to help me achieve the same result?' In other words, when something doesn't resonate, ask yourself: 'How can I make this work for me?' That's the question I always ask myself when something doesn't quite sit with me. So, I encourage you – be committed to the transformation and if a process doesn't work for you, change it.

Transformational Tools

OK, so let's get started. I'll be asking you to keep a journal throughout this process, as there's great power in writing your thoughts down, or, if you prefer, recording and playing them back to yourself as you go about your daily tasks. It's totally your choice which format to use, but for simplicity's sake, I'll refer to journaling, and writing your thoughts and feelings down throughout this book.

What if I told you that you never have to worry about not having enough ever again? Take a moment and ask yourself, 'How does that feel in my body?'

Really let it sink in. You might want to close your eyes and just notice how your body feels at the idea of never having to worry about not having enough or being enough ever again.

How did it feel? Calming? Relaxing? Peaceful? Expansive? Note it down in your journal.

I remember the first time I asked myself that question. It was like my entire body sighed. This is a question I invite you to keep coming back to. Whenever you're feeling stressed, lacking, or fearful about being able to receive what it is you desire, come back first to the question, and second to knowing that to receive infinitely is your birthright. Through these pages, you're not only going to remember that, but you are going to activate the frequency of receiving consciously. And this is going to change your experience of every moment of your life for as long as you choose to remember.

Maybe the idea of receiving consciously feels so far removed from where you are right now because you didn't access any of those feelings. Perhaps you noticed a numbness, or maybe you even felt constricted. If so, don't worry. This is exactly why you're here, and it's my intention that this book becomes the key to unlocking a whole new world of joy and abundance as we journey on this path together.

I'm so grateful and so excited to be able to share this with you. You're on the verge of creating something monumental in your life!

Suzy

Faith + Action = Miracles

Part I

Reimagining Your Perception of Wealth

Chapter 1

What Is Infinite Receiving?

When I first mention the words 'Infinite Receiving,' it's not unusual for people to experience a little tingle of excitement. I mean, the idea of being able to tune in and consciously choose and receive all that you desire – *infinitely* – is pretty sexy, right? Then, right after the tingle, many of those same people say, 'OK, but what exactly do we need to *do* to make it all happen? What are we talking about here?'

Infinite Receiving, as I alluded to in the Introduction, is a lifestyle and a philosophy for living. It's also a frequency that, when you're tapped into and energetically aligned with, unlocks a whole new world of joy, abundance, and ultimately – perhaps most importantly – a whole new level of peace. What's frequency, you may ask? In simple terms, everything is made out of energy, including our thoughts. The term 'frequency' refers to the speed at which the energy vibrates. This vibrational speed gives something its form, shape, color, sound, or texture. This is true for physical objects and gases – the frequency determines their characteristics. However, when it comes to thoughts and feelings, people are more likely to measure the frequency as either 'high' or 'low.' When you're tuned into the Infinite Receiving frequency, you're aligned with a mindset that helps you release the constant doubts about yourself and life, allowing you to live at a 'higher' frequency. By fully embracing and mastering this approach to living and thinking, you reach a point where you can create a life where you are operating from a place of peace and quiet confidence. You know what it feels like to trust and relax as you live your life knowing that you're fully supported in all that you do, across all areas of your life, and the world that you are living in unfolds for you, not against you, at all times.

I know this is a HUGE statement to make, especially if the environment that you are building a business or living in right now is challenging. If this is you, I want to ask you again to come on the journey with me anyway, and if by the end of the book you still feel that this is nonsense, you won't hear another peep out of me. While your life won't have changed if you see things in the exact same light as you do now, imagine if, through what you're about to read in these pages, you do begin to see things differently? And as you think about what this new and different perspective might look like, imagine you were able to create a whole new, wildly different and unexpected chapter in the story of your life. *What if...?*

And so, this journey has already begun.

Living your life from this perspective not only changes the game you're playing, but also has the capacity to change the 'game' for everyone you meet. It's impossible for it not to.

Why? Because as you see more and more 'magic' playing out in your life and your business, as you love the life you are living more, as you consciously co-create a world beyond what your mind previously thought was possible, the people around you won't be able to help but notice something's different.

Some people will ask you if you've had a haircut; others might say, 'Wow, you're glowing!' Some may simply comment on how happy you look, and you get to smile and receive everything they're saying, knowing exactly *why* they sense the changes in your life and in the way you now carry yourself.

If you have a business, you'll love it even more, as you'll find the courage to stop doing the things that don't align with your values. You'll stop selling products and services that no longer interest you, and you'll be honest about how you want to do business – how much you want to charge and how you desire to deliver – and actually have people respond positively to you. While this book isn't about the nuts and bolts of building a business, I'll share with you in these pages how this work has impacted both my clients and me, both in life and in business. And what it has done for me, I fully believe it can do for you, too.

We're going to talk about how you can get more of what it is that you desire in the coming pages, because everyone wants to know that bit. But truthfully, what you get materially through Infinite Receiving is a by-product of who you are *being*, what you are feeling, and what you are thinking about yourself. If I had to put into one sentence what the Infinite Receiving method is really about, I'd say it's increasing your state of awareness so that you can see more, feel more, and experience more... and, therefore, receive more.

Transformational Tools

Before we embark on the journey toward a new and elevated level of awareness, it's important to have a clear understanding of our starting point. The Wheel of Infinite Receiving (see also p.235) is a powerful tool that can help us in this process by providing a quick and measurable visual overview of where we stand in various aspects of our lives, such as love and relationships, health, spirituality, personal

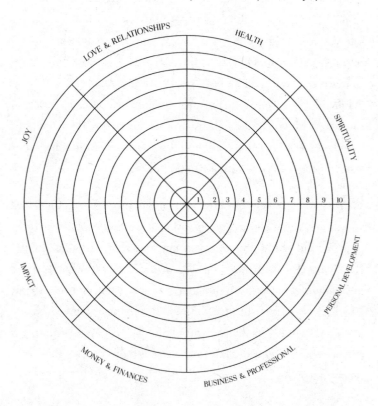

The Wheel of Infinite Receiving

development, business and professional life, money and finances, community and social impact, and personal joy.

The true power of this tool lies in its ability to inspire change. For example, if your current level of joy ranks at a 1 out of 10, instead of feeling deflated and demoralized by this, you can use the Wheel's concrete reference point as a motivator toward immediate action to raise that level to a 10. So, you get to choose a variety of things that bring you joy and to practice them consciously and consistently until, before you know it, your level of joy reaches, or even surpasses, a 10. Pretty cool, right?

Once we begin working on improving one or more areas, the beauty of the Wheel of Infinite Receiving becomes evident. It allows us to revisit it time and again to track our progress. I strongly encourage you to utilize this tool and witness the magic it can work for you. To begin, identify the top three areas you wish to focus on in the next 12 months. Whether it's health, spirituality, personal development, business, career, finances, or any others that resonate with you, rate your current position on a scale of 1 to 10 in each of these areas, shading them in with a pencil or colored pens if you prefer. Then, envision where you see yourself at the next level. (Your next level should feel like a stretch, but at the same time possible for you to achieve.) As you begin to take small, consistent actions toward reaching the next level in your chosen area(s), you'll be able to shade in more parts of the Wheel as your levels move closer and closer to a 10 in each area. This exercise will provide you with a clearer vision of where you can consciously direct your attention and expand your ability to receive.

My mission with this book is to empower you to increase your state of awareness on a consistent basis so that you can consciously create the life – and business, if that's your goal – of your dreams.

Once you've identified where you are and your next level, the next step (which sits alongside creating a consistent state of awareness) is the step of knowing who you are. That might sound like a funny thing to say, because of course you know who you are. The truth is, however, that most people have no idea that the person they are looking at in the mirror every day is a potent and powerful creator and receiver who's barely scratching the surface of what they are *truly* capable of receiving. So, that's what we'll look at next.

You are a creator, a manifestor, and a receiver.
When you learn how to create, allow, and receive
consistently, you can have anything you want.

Transformational Tools

We're going to be talking a lot about feelings and the energy that's created when you feel a certain way. I'll use the words 'energy' and 'frequency' interchangeably throughout the book. One of the most important energies

I want you to practice becoming aware of is the feeling that you get when you know that it's safe for you to stop worrying.

How do you do this? Don't be fooled by the simplicity of this, but I want you to repeat the following phrases:

'I am safe right now.'

'I am safe right now.'

'I am safe.'

What do you notice in your body? Does your body believe it? If it does, you're likely to feel a sense of calm and spaciousness. If not, you might feel tight and contracted. Next, I want you to imagine – just for the next few minutes – that all your problems, worries, concerns are going to be taken care of. Then say these affirmations again:

'I am safe right now.'

'I am safe right now.'

'I am safe.'

When your body believes you, you'll notice yourself relaxing. You'll sense more spaciousness in your chest, between your shoulders, and in your mind.

Now picture a person, a place, or an experience you love. Notice how using your mind in this way changes the feeling in the body again.

What sensations do you notice?

A warmth in your chest? A tingling in your toes? Perhaps you don't notice any changes in your body at all right now, or you might feel tightness in your body. That's OK, too, because we're just beginning to stretch your IR muscle. And that's exactly what it is: a muscle that must be exercised in order to be able to reach its full potential.

So, think of this book as your Infinite Receiving gym and this exercise as your first workout. Luckily for you, the motto 'no pain, no gain' is the absolute opposite of what we teach. That's not to say there won't be moments where you feel sad or uncomfortable - transformation is supposed to take us beyond our comfort zone in life. However, there's a way for you to dance between the discomfort and the growth in a manner that leaves you feeling energized and ready for more. And the energy field that this feeling generates is a magnet for magic. We'll keep coming back to this idea throughout the coming pages.

Getting the tingles

It's my desire that you notice more and more frequently how you *feel* and allow those feelings to show up without suppressing them. Why? Because your feelings and learning how to process those feelings – notice I used the word 'process' and not 'master,' not 'dominate,' not 'manipulate,' not 'control,' but 'process' your feelings – are your gateway to receiving more abundantly than you thought was possible.

Sometimes those feelings will feel icky and uncomfortable. That's OK, because on the other side of your more challenging feelings, such as guilt, shame, fear, unworthiness, and resentment, lies your most expansive self: the part of you that gets to be in love with life – even in its ordinary moments.

Want me to let you in on a little secret? It feels even more delicious when you *feel* the magic, especially when you're simply out for a walk in the park and the feeling of richness and the wealth of life consumes you from the inside out. Or you have a moment when you look at yourself in the mirror *before* you've got dressed up and are ready to go out and you notice a radiance illuminating every part of your face.

When you feel the tingles when you're doing even the most mundane of tasks, you'll know that you have consciously activated the Infinite Receiving frequency, because you feel full just by being yourself. Adding the sprinkles on top, such as incredible experiences or getting the things you've always wanted, can be great. However, it's important to recognize that these 'extras' can't diminish the wholeness and contentment that already exist within you. This is what I mean by doing the work from the inside out.

Question – does safety come before the tingles, or is it the tingles that create the safety?

As your teachers should have always told you – safety first. Although, in my experience, I might not consciously be aware that I am, in fact, feeling safe before the tingles set in. But from a neurological perspective, safety creates the space for you to release the feel-good hormones dopamine and serotonin, which in turn generate a blissful or peaceful sense of contentment.

Many people think that they'll feel safe when they have X amount of money in the bank. That's a lie. True safety and security come from within and have nothing to do with our external circumstances. I know that might feel challenging to accept, but when a person feels truly safe, they are able to find that feeling amid all the chaos and drama of life – partners coming and going, clients defaulting on payments, things not going to plan. And when we feel safe in the knowledge that not only are we OK, but we're going to be OK *regardless* of whether we win or lose this next roll of the dice – this is when we're at our most powerful. And it's this deep sense of inner security that empowers us to create the life we truly desire.

I invite you, if you feel comfortable to do so, to try this 'I am Limitless Meditation.' It's about planting the seeds, reminding yourself who you are and that you're limitless. And in your limitlessness, which touches every single corner of this universe, everything that you desire is here. Right here and now.

This is an *ahh-maz-ing* exercise for opening your heart space. You can listen to it in the *Empower You Unlimited Audio* app – go to the App Store or Google Play to download it and then search for 'Meditations for Infinite Receiving.' Or, if you prefer, you can record it in your own voice and play it back.

Transformational Tools

Sit comfortably and, if it feels good and safe for you to do so, I invite you just to allow your eyes to gently close. Focus on your breath for a moment or so.

Allow your energy field to settle... maybe you want to put your hand on your heart, feel it beating, and imagine it pumping the blood around the body. Perhaps you feel more comfortable just resting your hands on your thighs, palms upward, in receiving mode. Just find your highest alignment, that connection with your best self, as we open this portal – open this experience – together.

I invite you now to bring your attention to the spaciousness within your body. Just notice where you can feel the space and, as you bring your attention to the space within your body, as you breathe in, allow that space to expand, creating more room, more space.

Perhaps you've noticed areas where there's tightness and it feels like constriction within the body. I invite you to allow your awareness to focus its attention on those spaces. And I invite you to breathe space into those areas. And all you have to do is just notice even the smallest of changes as you bring your attention to the shoulders, the neck, the shoulder blades, perhaps to the hips. Just notice wherever there's tightness. Breathe spaciousness.

Roll the shoulders back. Open the heart space. And notice the spaciousness around the heart and breathe. As you notice the spaciousness around the heart, I invite you to bring your awareness to the center of the heart...

... and I wonder how quickly you can begin to notice just the smallest of flames. Just notice, with every inhalation, how that flame in the center of the heart gets a little bigger. With every breath in, it's getting a little bigger and bigger until that flame is lighting up the whole of your heart...

... and you're able to just notice the space outside of the heart and the light within the heart, both expanding with every inhalation and just a small contraction with every exhalation. The deeper you breathe, the bigger the flame and the bigger the space.

Just notice, too, how that spaciousness moves throughout the entire body and invite the light to fill all the space.

And then, bringing your attention to the outside of your body, notice the space that goes beyond your energy field. Visualize the space within the field and the space without. Become aware of both areas as you picture yourself sitting, like a shining ball of light, in the middle of both the space within and the space without.

Now I invite you to just allow both your awareness and your energy to move into the room around you. And so again, you're noticing the space within, the space without, and the light within. And you're just allowing that light within the space within to move into the space without, filling the entire room that you're in.

Notice how your body feels as you allow yourself to expand more and more into the room that you're in. Now allow that expansion to move beyond the room, into the road outside of the home or the place where you're sitting right now – your energy, your spaciousness, your expansiveness moving into the village or the town. Allow your awareness to notice yourself in every nook and cranny…

… your expansiveness is getting bigger and bigger with every inhalation: the space within filling the space without – into the county or the state that you're in, into the country that you're in, filling, expanding into every part of it. Allow yourself to be as expansive as you desire. Perhaps you want to go around the entire world right now. Don't think, just allow. Perhaps you go into the universe, into space; your spaciousness within and without goes into space and that light fills every nook and cranny, getting bigger and bigger and bigger.

Just notice how the body feels as you expand and expand and expand. And there's a part of you that already knows that everything that you desire is currently being touched by your field of energy. Everything that you have ever desired, everything that you will ever desire, everything that you currently desire is being touched by your energy field. It's already there.

Without being specific, I invite you just to allow yourself to tune in to the frequency that feels the strongest when it comes to your alignment with the manifestation that you desire. Don't be specific. Just allow my words to allow you to continue to expand while aligning.

Notice how you feel as you allow yourself to align to the manifestation that's desiring to come through to you now. Notice how you feel. Notice how your body feels. Observe without any judgment - just allow yourself to align to the frequency of the manifestation that's ready to come through to you in this moment.

I invite you to take a slow, deep breath in. Hold the breath for a moment and then exhale audibly. Notice how you feel. Notice the still-expanded state of awareness and note consciously and subconsciously how it feels to be in this expanded state of awareness - this elevated state of consciousness.

Now what I invite you to do is just call all your energy back into your solar plexus - the chakra just above the belly button. Call it all in, call it all back to you, so you're not scattered around the universe. Don't be alarmed by this - know that your intention is enough to call it all back to you in an instant. But if you find it helpful, you can visualize golden rays of light flooding back into your solar plexus, or you can say out loud: 'I call all of my energy back in from all times, spaces, and dimensions' and it will be done.

As you call the energy back, notice how you can still maintain that elevated state of awareness, that elevated state of expansiveness.

Notice the soles of your feet on the floor - feel roots coming out of the base of your soles, anchoring you into the Earth beneath you, so you are fully, completely here on solid ground. And whenever you're ready, and not a moment before, just allow your eyes to gently open, coming back fully present to the here and the now.

Notice how you feel right now. Then list your feelings and any other thoughts in your journal.

~ Q&A ~

Q: *What do we need to do in order to be able to receive?*

A: I want to make this distinction: We're all receiving, 24 hours a day, seven days a week, whether we want to accept it or not — we're always in receiving mode. But, to consciously receive what we desire, we're going to need to start with releasing fear, shame, guilt, and judgment.

Faith + Action = Miracles

Chapter 2

Wanting More
vs. Greed

One thing people often mention to me when I talk about Infinite Receiving is their concern that it promotes greed. They worry that wanting more for more's sake is just wrong, especially when you don't have to look beyond the latest headline to see the undeniable inequity in the world.

This is true. And yet…

The desire for more is innate within us all. It's programmed into our DNA. We first recognize this impulse by observing babies. As long as they are physically able to, the baby on their back on the floor becomes curious about the world around them and it's as if they go, 'I want to sit up. I want to be able to see more.' And as babies ourselves, as we were able to, we writhed and wriggled and demanded all the assistance we could get, until we too could sit up. Then, observing objects and people across the room, we discovered crawling as a means of getting ourselves from A to

B, perhaps in search of a rattle or other shiny thing. We learned to stand. Then to walk. The desire to evolve and want more has always been there.

Where this intrinsic part of our nature has been distorted is through marketing that preys on our fears about our inaccurately perceived 'inadequacies.' Our desire for more because we're born creators was weaponized and used against us, with the lie that if we just get this one more thing, then we'll feel better about who we are; then our parents will love us or see us; then we'll be worthy of love; then we'll feel safe. Wanting more so we can feel safe and lovable will never fulfil our deepest desires. And you won't be surprised to learn that from this space, the pursuit of wanting more is a big, fat NO.

In case you haven't noticed, Infinite Receiving comes from a completely different starting point. It 100 percent helps you boost the money in your bank account, but it goes beyond that. It's designed to help you experience a profound sense of abundance in your heart, your mind, and your soul. Personally, I discovered on my own journey to embracing wealth in every aspect of my life that I first had to be honest with what I wanted before I could receive it. Believe it or not, however, that question – what you want – for so many people, is a challenging and often scary one to answer truthfully.

Why? Because when a person is willing to get honest about what it is they *actually* want from their life, it frequently highlights where they have been tolerating less than what they want – perhaps because it feels safer; because they don't feel worthy of the things they desire; because they are afraid that everything they have built will fall away if they are real with themselves. Which is why this journey isn't always an easy one.

But hear me when I say that on the other side of your discomfort, if you're willing to do the work, is a life beyond what you thought was possible for you. My clients and I are living proof of it.

~ **Affirmation** ~

Repeat this (and all the affirmations in this book that resonate with you) out loud:

It's my time. I am ready. I am ready to rise. I am ready to receive.

A little about me

I think it's easy to look at someone who has outwardly and materially reached a level of success, and to think things like:

- 'Well, it's all right for you.'

- 'You would say that!'

- 'What would you know?'

And it's true. In my business, I talk frequently not just about being in the top 1 percent of the world for income earners, but also how much that statistic means to me. On paper, it shouldn't be me sharing these truths and living this life. Not just because I'm a dark-skinned Black woman (although that has a little to do with why I say it shouldn't be me) but also because when you consider that I was placed into foster care when I was just three months old, my story could have been very different. At that time in the UK, it was normal for Nigerian parents to use private foster carers to look after their children while they worked to send money back to extended family abroad. My biological parents decided that this route was going to be the best for them and found the woman who I grew up calling Mum in the back of a magazine. Can you imagine?

I feel extremely fortunate to say that I got lucky. Very lucky. Because, while that household didn't have very much money, there was plenty of love. Mum was a cleaner and earned a side income through a network marketing organization called Avon. 'Avon ladies' would go door to door, popping the product magazine through letter boxes, return a few days later to collect the magazines and the order forms, and earn a commission from the orders they would then receive and deliver to their loyal customers. My dad was an odd-job man at the local paint factory. My parents worked really hard, for very little, but when I reflect on it, it's there the seeds for *Infinite Receiving* were first sown.

My mum was the type of person to make s*** happen. She never really had the money for luxuries, but she made things happen. Mainly, she wasn't too embarrassed to ask for what she needed or what we wanted. It meant that even though we had the worst car out of all my friends and lived in the smallest bungalow, in which I shared a bedroom with my younger sister, when I wanted to do things, her attitude – their attitude, my mum and my dad – was always, 'Why not? Give us a minute, and we'll get it sorted.' It meant that we got grants so I could learn how to play the flute and the cello. I went on the school ski trip with the help of a school bursary. Once, my mum even won a trolley dash, which meant we were able to stock up on a load of extras just before Christmas and, while I don't remember exactly what we got, I remember the exhilaration of finding out that we had won and that I was going to be the one running around the supermarket pushing the trolley. We lived on many handouts and a lot of love.

While I didn't see my biological parents from the ages of eight to 18 years old, and moved out of the bungalow for the first time aged 17, what really changed the trajectory of my life was when my foster mother died of cancer when I was 19. Although I was living independently at that point, my life was pretty messy. I had dropped out of college, I was smoking a lot of weed, drinking, and doing more than my fair share of recreational drugs. For work, I found myself behind the bar in my local pub and working at an array of the city's pizza restaurants. I was going nowhere fast.

When I found out my mum was sick, I visited her in hospital once and the experience deeply affected me. Seeing her so unwell and how frail she looked was incredibly distressing. She just kept saying, 'I've got to see you get married.' It was so upsetting that I never went back. It's the biggest regret of my life. Not being able to provide support to the woman who had shown me immense love and care and support throughout my formative years, failing in that moment to grasp the significance of just how ill she was, and being absent in her time of need still haunts me today. I was young and selfish. My foster mother died on 1 December, 1997. I was devastated.

Experiencing loss at that time of my life, ironically, turned out to be my greatest gift and my biggest lesson, and it continues to teach me and show me just how much more I have to learn every single day.

If you had told 19-year-old Suzy that one day she would run a thriving multi-million-pound business, dedicated to helping people all over the world achieve their dreams, all while raising three children and finding profound happiness – even after the end of a 15-year relationship with their father (with whom she co-parents successfully) – I'd probably have used a swear word. Similarly, if you had told me that I'd have Sir Richard Branson's telephone number at my fingertips, be writing my second book, be invited to speak on international stages, I'd have told you not to be ridiculous. And if you had told me that I'd have a genuinely happy heart, I know I wouldn't have believed you.

When I tell you that I transformed myself from that selfish, self-centered 19-year-old who couldn't even get a promotion in a pizza restaurant into who I am today, I truly mean it. And let me assure you, if I can achieve this transformation, so can you.

From great to exceptional

So, what if your life is already pretty freaking amazing? Who are you to say that you want more? The truth is, if you are already wildly, deeply, and madly in love with yourself and have everything you desire materially, you're right – you don't need to read another word. Give yourself a pass and go on with your life.

But if you're feeling like it's not fair for you to ask for more because you already have so much, I want to say, you having more does not take away from anyone else. In fact, it's quite the opposite. When

YOU have MORE than enough... you have more to give, and you have more to create with. And, as we saw on pp.4–5, when you live from a place of abundance in your daily life, even your presence has a transformative effect on those around you. So, get ready for a flood of compliments from friends, acquaintances, family, and complete strangers, because I'm telling you – *everyone* will notice your 'glow.' This radiance doesn't come from what you own, but rather is a reflection of your authentic self – who you are *being*.

Super exciting, right?

I hope this inspires you to imagine a world where people truly know that they're whole, complete, and enough whenever they step out of their front doors each day, commute to work, or sit in front of their computer screens. How would the world change if people stopped wanting from a place of feeling unworthy and started choosing and creating from a place of overflow? And how different would you feel if you saw someone's radiance and, instead of feeling 'less-than' or 'not enough,' knew that it was possible for you to radiate like that too? How different would this world be?

> *Most people are trying to fill themselves up*
> *with their manifestations, and wondering why,*
> *even when they are successful, they still feel*
> *hungry? Create from a place of fullness versus*
> *filling yourself, and see the magic unfold.*

What you need to know

As we continue on our journey together, there are a few principles we need to embed in our minds to help shift our thinking from believing that wanting more is inherently wrong or greedy to knowing at our core that there is enough for everyone, and that wanting more is not only OK, but something to celebrate. You'll discover how each of the following empowers you to receive and manifest abundance in every aspect of your life. Here are the key takeaways:

1. *You are whole. You are worthy and complete. Right now.*

If you only take one thing from this book and this principle is the one thing that you choose to work on knowing to be true, it will change your entire life. Understanding our wholeness is integral to our understanding of the Four Pillars of Infinite Receiving and is one of the key fundamentals that underpin the process. So, let's explore this further:

There is no separation

This principle applies to multiple things in multiple ways. At a basic level, the way a person feels about themselves and the world carries its own unique energetic signature. This is experienced by everyone who comes into contact with it and holds true whether they consciously know it or not. No matter how much a person attempts to isolate themselves from friends, family, or the world in general, how they feel can be felt, because, as the law of conservation of energy makes clear, energy can't be created or destroyed, merely transferred or transmuted.

I've come to realize that although each person's life circumstances influence their journey and, in some cases, make it easier to accomplish certain things, one belief that has always empowered me on my own journey is simply this: *Why not me?* When I saw people doing the things that I desired to do and showing up in the world in the way that I desired to *be*, instead of looking for the things that were different between those people and me, I started looking for things that were similar. Finding the evidence to support the possibility of achieving my desires. I stopped creating barriers, removed the pedestals I'd put people on, and allowed myself to notice all the places where we were the same or similar. I embraced these similarities as proof that I, too, could achieve what I longed for. If other successful people could achieve their goals, why couldn't I do the same? Why not me?

This principle has set me free so many times, and it can do the same for you.

The other thing I want you to truly understand is the idea that there's no separation between you and all the things you desire. We will learn more about this in detail in the Pillar of Infinite Conscious Creation chapter (p.207) but, for now, know that there is no separation between you and me, between you and anything.

My response determines my experience

When we're living our everyday lives, there are literally millions of external elements that are taking place completely outside of our field of awareness and control every second. The way we respond to the circumstances we do control will determine the quality of our lives and our daily experience. When we're willing to take radical responsibility for the way we respond to life, it's amazing how much more quickly we can forgive, love, be open, and, ultimately, be in the position to receive more of what we actually want.

Taking responsibility for the way I respond to life empowers me. It means I get to choose.

2. *Claiming isn't enough*

I meet so many people who've been told that they've just got to name and claim what it is that they want – *just name it and claim it!*

Let me tell you, naming and claiming a thing isn't enough. You also have to feel it in your body as though it were already done. This is called *embodiment.* And you have to know it. You have to *know* that the thing you want is yours.

I want you to do more than just think, wish, or dream about it. Many people reach this point and stop, never understanding why they never quite achieve what they desire – whether it's a new deal, a big client, a promotion, a pay rise, a fulfilling relationship, or forgiveness. I invite you to move 'beyond your brain' and connect with the feelings of already having what you desire within your body. It's by truly feeling and knowing it that you become a match for it (or something even better) and its manifestation is inevitable.

~ Affirmation ~

I am happy and excited about being a match for more and knowing there's so much more to come.

How you show up

As you go through each chapter, start tuning into your body, paying attention to how you're feeling. Notice when you feel your heart expand for no particular reason. Or feel blissful for no particular reason. Not because the sun is the most beautiful color that you've ever seen, or the sky is magnificent. Literally, for no reason.

Notice when you feel the joy of being yourself. The joy of consciously choosing to evolve and getting to know yourself as you live even more deeply into your potential.

Notice when you are able to feel and maintain the feeling of excitement about the next great thing that's coming in. Even when you're not quite sure what it is or even when it's coming, but you trust that it is coming.

Notice when the need to push, to grab, to work it out dissipates. Because there's something coming through that's undeniable.

Undeniable. This is what I'm talking about. When you are tapped into Infinite Receiving, it's about knowing at every moment that you're receiving a lesson. A gift. Wisdom. Something that gets to enrich every single freaking moment of your existence in a way that will blow your mind.

Remember, we're all already infinitely receiving. It's true! But not everyone can currently feel it. Not everyone can see it. I want you to feel it. I want you to see it in the most exquisite way. And then I want you to start consciously co-creating with it.

So, we know that the mission of Infinite Receiving is to create a whole new way of experiencing life for you when it comes to working, playing, creating, and receiving. And that this method has the capacity to change not just your life, but the lives of every single person that you touch, and then every single person that they touch.

But we're not just talking about different, more abundant lives; we're talking about a raise in the consciousness of this planet, which is absolutely required at this time in this world. We owe it to ourselves and each other to get into the flow of Infinite Receiving and stay there!

Transformational Tools

To finish this chapter, I invite you to try the following exercise. Answer the following question in your journal:

> What are the fears you have around being a person who is able to create exactly what you desire?

And I want you to look at your answers, as if you were having a face-to-face with yourself.

Then, one by one, I want you to notice over our time together, how you just choose to release each fear.

I want you to notice when you're playing into the old identity, the one who's afraid, and I want you to make new decisions.

I want you to make different choices. You can do this.

~ Q&A ~

Q: *You were talking about feeling the next level. So, first feeling energetically in our body what we want to call in before it comes into the physical, and I was like, 'What the hell is she talking about? How does that even feel?' Well, I've now got that. I can feel that something big is coming – I don't know what it is yet, I can't put my finger on it – but it's amazing. My question is twofold: obviously there's this trust that I've never had before, but is it one specific thing or a combination? And, when you can feel this trust, do you hold it or try to expand it?*

A: It's a combination of things and that's really important. It's always layered – never just one thing. It's a combination of many little things that you've been doing that have created shifts in your reality. And now you have something coming in. You're not quite sure what it is, but you can feel it. You're better able to feel it because of the shifts that you have made. And with your question about trust, the answer is: both. I hold it and expand it. I ask myself, 'How much more can I feel it? How much more can I allow it?'

Faith + Action = Miracles

Chapter 3

Fundamentals of Conscious Wealth Expansion

So, if the first step was making peace with the idea of having more, the second step is understanding what it means to consciously create a whole new level of abundance – specifically, wealth. And it is my belief that the planet needs many more conscious, wealthy human beings, like you. Conscious, wealthy people with a desire to create and receive more so that they can do good, not only for themselves and their families, but for the world. Wealthy, conscious leaders who want to make the decisions that impact everyone, for the highest good of all.

Sounds like utopia? Maybe. But the journey to better for everyone begins with one conscious wealthy person at a time. And this starts with understanding the different types of wealth that contribute to you being a truly wealthy person.

The breakdown

Wealth, from the perspective of Infinite Receiving, is made up of three different elements: intrinsic, experiential, and leverageable wealth – the Trifecta. All three are equally important and uniquely separate. The problem arises when we combine and attach these three areas to each other, creating a big, messy, and chaotic relationship with wealth – be it attracting, generating, or keeping it.

- **Intrinsic wealth** is all about how worthy and how rich you feel on the inside, along with your own sense of safety. *Do I feel rich, safe, and secure regardless of my external circumstances, no matter what's going on around me?*

- **Experiential wealth** is your experience of the good life, your lifestyle, and life design. It's your ability and the freedom you have to choose what it is that you truly want, without needing to hold back. It's you consciously designing and living the experience of a rich life.

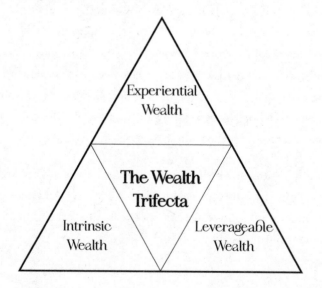

- **Leverageable wealth** is the money piece of the equation. How much money you have in your bank account and how easy it is for you to make and accumulate money.

For you to create more wealth across all areas of your life, it's useful to look at each of the pillars of the Trifecta. This will show you where you get to choose to redefine your relationship with wealth, within the context of the Trifecta, and where you get to amplify the things that are already working to put you in the best possible position for activating Infinite Receiving across all areas of your life.

For me, the really juicy part is that, as you go through this process, you'll get to reimagine and redefine what it means to be wealthy in the most nourishing and liberating ways.

In my experience, especially in working with people in the business world, the number-one focus when trying to create more abundance generally is leverageable wealth. In other words, it's about finding ways to get more money in your bank account. Seems perfectly logical, right? However, completely counter-intuitively, it rarely produces the desired effect.

The story that I hear most often is, 'When I make the money, then I'll be less stressed and happier; I'll feel safe and secure.' Or: 'When I receive the money, I'll have the evidence that I'm worthy and that I'm deserving.' Most people believe that leverageable wealth is the gateway to intrinsic and experiential wealth. What I've seen time and time again is that in order to be and feel *truly* wealthy across all areas of your life, you can't just focus on the money. Leverageable wealth isn't a gateway to peace and well-being.

By the same token, while having feelings of safety and security and feeling worthy and deserving on the inside is freaking amazing, if you want to have an impact in the world, whether that's working with and influencing millions of people or giving your children choices and opportunities, it's not just about the intrinsic wealth either; you also have to understand how you get to utilize leverageable wealth. You can absolutely be living your best life in your RV and feeling that you are having the greatest time ever. But if you have no idea how to create leverageable wealth, either through yourself or through others, you'll find it way more challenging to create the impact you want.

∼ Affirmation ∼

In my world, I get to do what I love. I get to receive the highest compensation financially, emotionally, spiritually, energetically.

Either/or thinking

One of the biggest challenges that people have to overcome when creating more wealth and abundance in their lives is the story that it needs to be one thing or the other. I can have the relationship, but I can't have the money. Or, if I choose the money, I will have to sacrifice my life because I'll have to work a lot harder. Set yourself free from this by holding on to the fact that, when it comes to the Wealth Trifecta, you don't have to choose one thing or the other, you get to choose *and*. You get to have the life *and* the business *and* the playtime *and* the family time. If that's what you want, you can absolutely choose that.

I'm passionate about this because, at the moment, there are too many people thinking that they don't have the capacity to work on all three areas of wealth expansion – intrinsic, experiential, and leverageable – at once. They think it's too much for them. They think that they have to choose just one thing, but they don't.

It doesn't always feel easy, but you can totally work on all three areas of the Trifecta at once. That's what so many conscious wealthy people are choosing to do. It's not a question of building the business or career they want *or* having the life they want. They are consciously choosing to have it all as they work on all three aspects of the Wealth Trifecta. This is absolutely what I recommend. How? You've already started with this book.

Transformational Tools

I'd love for you to try this next exercise.

Think about a moment in the past year when you felt deeply, deeply grateful. Perhaps it was something that happened to you, or maybe to someone that you love. Either way, pick a moment that makes you feel gratitude, joy, appreciation, not in your head - as in, don't think about it, *feel* it - but in your body. If you can't think of anything in the past year, then go back two years. Pick any moment in time.

I invite you to close your eyes and imagine yourself in the space that you were in at that time. Think about the sounds that you could hear, the look on your face or the face of the person that you are thinking about. Remember how it felt in your body, now. Allow yourself to revisit all the goodness and the lushness of that moment in the present moment.

Now, I don't want you to overthink this, but I want you to take a couple of minutes to write down in your journal what you just experienced. How did it feel in your body? What could you hear, what could you see? Capture as much as possible.

Consider how you felt. Did it feel good?

And how did your body respond? Did you feel warm, tingly, tearful (in a good way)?

While it's super OK if you didn't feel any of those things, this is a muscle that you get to strengthen over time. What you actually did there was something quite magical. Through using your imagination, you were able to recreate the same experience in the body that you had in the past, but in the here and now. And from a neurological perspective your brain has no idea that what you just recreated was a past memory and not actually happening in the moment.

As you learn to activate your Infinite Receiving code more intentionally, you'll experience firsthand the immense power of this tool you already possess and know how to use. You'll understand its potential to help you create more than you might even be able to imagine.

This is important because by simply revisiting past memories and recreating them in the present moment, you tap into your nature as a multidimensional human being. As well as being able to summon memories and feelings into the present moment from your past, you'll start consciously creating what you desire. It's an incredibly powerful tool. By tapping into your emotions related to the past and the future, you begin to discover the true expansiveness of your present moment. You don't need to go anywhere physically; it's about exploring how deeply and expansively you can allow yourself to *feel* right here and now. This awareness of expansive versus contracted energy is excellent when it comes to consciously co-creating and receiving what we desire.

What's interesting is that most people are doing this *all* the time unconsciously. Instead of tapping into high-frequency memories and experiences and imprinting those blueprints into their present-day reality, they are imprinting memories and experiences that make them less of a match for what they want and more of a match for what they don't. As they worry and feel anxious about what might be coming or feel guilty and embarrassed about the past, they are tuning into the lower frequencies that invite more of these feelings into their daily reality. We've all heard the saying 'you attract what you think about' and it's true. You're still in receiving mode when you are doing this – it's just not conscious.

What's special about that little exercise is that it's a reminder that you are a multidimensional human being – which in my book is pretty cool. What I mean is that even though you can be here in the moment, you can also travel back in time to a previous experience – recreating all your feelings, emotions, and goodness, creating an imprint of that in the here and now, amplifying your energetic field in the most positive ways, while increasing your field of awareness.

This is important because the people who are best equipped to receive more are the people who are able to see more of life. It's as though their peripheral vision has expanded and they're aware of there being so much more available to them.

So, are you open and available to widening the lens you use when it comes to your wealth?

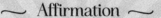

~ Affirmation ~

What I understand from the deepening of my own development is that you must be willing to see things differently. Use the following affirmation to help increase your awareness/abundance/lens of the world:

I am willing to see things differently.

Identity shift

One of the biggest things that I've worked on, and continue to work on every single day, is the constant and continual shifting of my identity. How we see ourselves determines our experiences, for better or worse. Our self-image influences what we allow into our lives, our perception of worthiness, and how much we believe we deserve.

It wasn't until I set up my own business that I realized how much the idea of having more than enough – of anything, but particularly money – felt not just alien, but scary to me. The story that I grew up with, the thing that I observed, was always that we only ever had 'just enough.' And just enough was great. On just enough, you could be happy. This is where I learned that *need* was the benchmark. If you didn't need it, then it wasn't necessary, and what's true is that it really wasn't necessary. As a family we lived a very happy life on 'just enough.'

I saw this play out in my business for years: the more I earned, the more I'd spend, leaving me with 'just enough' at the end of the month. Always enough, but always *just*.

And the reason I felt uncomfortable with allowing myself to be in overflow (not just receiving more, but keeping more) is because of what I believed at the time to be true about rich people and money in general.

In order to create change, you have to
be willing to see things differently.

Transformational Tools

Grab your journal and a pen and complete the following sentence, writing down as many things as you can think of:

Rich people are_____.

Keep going until you really feel complete.

What are some of the negative stories you learned about wealth and money when you were growing up?

Again, write down as many of the stories as you can remember.

When it came to stories and beliefs I had about rich people, wealth, and money, it was pretty clear why it didn't feel safe or right for me to be receiving in abundance. What's also interesting is how many of those limiting beliefs also showed up in my relationships, and in the way I viewed and received love. 'Just enough' was good enough in the reality I was unconsciously creating. Do you get the same clarity from the stories you have identified for yourself?

When we say yes to living a life of Infinite Receiving, we're also saying yes to viewing life differently and, more importantly, viewing ourselves differently. So, the question is, are you willing to step into a bigger vision for yourself? And when I say big, I mean a more expanded vision of the life you are living right now.

When you fully embrace this concept of Infinite Receiving, to begin with your vision expands. You start to ask yourself empowering questions like, 'What if this were possible for me? What if we could create that? What if I could allow that into my life? What if?' And as you start to say yes to living your life as though those what-ifs are really possible, you're going to notice an increase in your ability to be more courageous in your choices and decisions. The desire to sit on the fence will decrease and you'll begin to choose more in alignment with the vision you have for yourself and your future. And as you consciously create in your life and in your business, you'll notice what were once dreams actually showing up in your business and in your life. Little by little.

As you start to collect more and more evidence of what's possible, you'll notice your awareness and your entire field of vision increase. Answers to more of the questions you have will flow to you more effortlessly. Solutions in the shape of people, ideas, creative 'itches,' and nudges will start presenting themselves, as if by magic. A whole new level of wealth – across all areas of your life – will be activated.

To shift your perspective and fully embrace the affirmation, 'I am willing to see things differently' with all your being, we need to reprogram your thinking and the way you feel about some of the old, no-longer-useful stories and beliefs you carry that are blocking your capacity to receive more.

In the journal exercise we did earlier, if you answered, 'rich people are greedy,' that's impacting your wealth. If you wrote, 'rich people are beyond my reach,' that's impacting your capacity to live a rich life. So, I want you to recognize where your mind creates a limitation that stops you receiving in each of the areas of conscious wealth expansion.

Transformational Tools

Let's try another little exercise that might help make things clearer. Describe in your journal what the next level of wealth in your life might look like. What would it feel like? This is about looking at your life experience – your experiential wealth. Let's get specific. If the next level of wealth represents 'ease and freedom' to you, where will you experience more ease and freedom in your life? If that next level means to you more choice or greater companionship, where are you going to experience that in your life and how is it going to feel? What does more companionship look like to you? More time away from your desk? More holidays? What would you choose for you?

Once you've given these ideas some thought, the next question is: how do you know that you're not there yet? How do you know that you're not at the next level of wealth yet? What tangible experiences are you unable to access because you're not living at your next level of wealth in your life?

So, if you're looking for companionship, you might often feel lonely. But once you receive the companionship you desire, you might feel more joyful, happy, and relaxed.

If you're not sure where to start, focus on the three core areas you identified when you completed the Wheel of Infinite Receiving on p.6. Thinking about each area, and then what you'd like each to look like will help you to deep-dive on what the next level of wealth is specifically going to look like for you. I know you aren't there yet, because you've just identified the reasons that are holding you back. So, the big question is: how do we get to that next level of wealth?

And the answer is that it starts with a decision.

> *Every future success you will experience*
> *starts with a decision.*

A crucial decision

How many times have you made a decision about something in the past, and not seen it come to fruition? If you're anything like me, the answer will be more than a few times, I'm sure. The other thing I'm sure of is that every successful outcome you have ever experienced in your life started with you deciding to make it happen. So why are you able to pull it off sometimes, but not others? I'm going to show you and I'm going to make you feel better about all the times it hasn't worked out in the past. And guess what? All those times it didn't work weren't your fault. You'll have noticed that I talk a lot about things in threes. And I'm going to do it again. When it comes to making a decision, there are three layers of choice. Most people, when making a decision, home in on the outer layer, which is focused on results. So, what is it that you want to achieve? For example, to promote your business and generate clients, you want to host your first live event. OK, so you decide that's what you want to achieve.

The outer layer is the result – the live event.

Then you go to the second layer, and you ask yourself, 'What do I need to do to get that result? What's the system? What process is required in order to get that result? *How* do I get there?'

You need to market and sell tickets to the event. This is the secondary layer – the process.

And then we have the inner layer – who you need to be in order to create the result you desire. This is your identity. There's an amazing quote from James Clear, who talks about this in his book, *Atomic Habits*, that says, 'behavior that is incongruent with the self will not last.' Your identity is your Self.

As we've noted, most people usually try to make changes from the outside in, and focus primarily on the *result*, closely followed by the process or the strategy to get the result. However, for you to make a shift that actually changes things, you must work from the inner layer first and create a shift in your identity so you can become the type of person who gets the results you actually want. The questions to ask yourself, then, are: 'Who do I need to be? What do I need to believe?'

If you change your beliefs, you can change your results. Of course, you'll still need a *process* and a *system* to help you achieve your outcomes, but the real reason goal-setting often fails is that most of the time, people are working from the outside layer in – result-focused first – rather than from the inner layer out, starting with the identity piece.

It's so easy to see this when we look at a person who's trying to receive more money or be in a new relationship. If a person believes that they're not worthy and deserving of receiving more, the best business strategy in the world won't provide sustained results. And it is the same with love. If you don't believe deep down that you are worthy of an incredible 'write-a-movie-about-it' love affair, then you're likely to settle for partners who don't align with where you are headed, or who aren't a good match for you long term. You end up settling for less than what you actually desire.

How do we know when we've really made a decision?

You might be thinking, 'I get this, but I've made decisions hundreds of times and thought about who I need to be many, many times before in my past and I still haven't got the result that I want. Why is that?' It's a good question, and the key to your answer lies in your behaviors.

Making a decision with your mind is one thing, and I know you know that. *You know you know that.* Making a decision with your head isn't the same as following through with your way of being – having your heart and your behaviors line up with the decision, too. If you want to create a true identity shift, you must be willing not just to think about things differently, you must be willing to DO things differently and have your behavior back up the words that are coming out of your mouth. Otherwise, they really are 'just words.'

Time for some real talk: When you think about some of the things you have been *saying* are important in your life – building a world-class business, getting a new job, deepening the relationships you have with the people that mean the most to you, being a match for a new love – look at how you have been *speaking* about the shift you want to create. We all know that our words hold power. Are you talking like the type of person who knows that they are a match for being the founder of a business that is changing lives and being spoken about by people worldwide? Are you talking as though you know that you are actually ready – now – for the love of your life to sweep in and meet you mentally, emotionally, and physically? Are you talking as though you are ready to find that new home you've long dreamed about? Or are you wishing about it, hoping about it, would kind of like it, but not sure that now would even be the best time for it, anyway? Would absolutely love it, but don't want to get your hopes up too much, in case it doesn't happen for a while, or maybe even at all...?

When you look at your actions – do they also align with the actions of the type of person who has, or is creating, what you want to create? Or are you behaving in the same way you have always behaved and doing what you have always done – which is to get all excited about a new good habit for a week or two, maybe even a month or two, and the longer you don't see the physical evidence of the thing you want coming to fruition, the more your enthusiasm fizzles out. And the more time passes without seeing tangible results, the more you gradually lose momentum, or even stop taking the necessary actions to achieve what those who already possess the things you say you desire *actually do.*

This happens because on the inside, the identity that you most align with, which of course doesn't have the thing and is not worthy of the result, doesn't really need it. The old identity is still running the show. Which is why most people fall before they cross the finish line and achieve their goals.

Upgrading what you have the capacity to receive and be a match for takes upgrading your beliefs and frequently (but not always) the contexts and experiences you put yourself into to create sustained change. And while it's true that instantaneous shifts *can* happen (I know, because I've experienced them and seen many over the years), big transformations, aka quantum shifts, usually happen over time. Because even when the penny finally drops on the things we need to change, the outward results are the almost always the last thing we see. It takes time for the inevitable outcome to catch up with the shift in your identity. But what I can promise you is that after you have started to apply this shift in thinking and being, you are going to get really good at recognizing the feeling you get in your body, when you just KNOW something is done, way before the evidence presents itself. And that's when the fun and games really begin.

'But I want it and I want it *now*,' I hear some of you say. I get it. Frequently, especially in the online business world, the stories that sell the most courses, product, or service, are the 'miracle' stories, where there has been a massive change over a really short period. An instantaneous quantum shift in somebody's world, finances, relationships, health, weight, or well-being. While these are fun to read about, frequently these stories are anomalies – that's why they stand out. They don't happen all the time, even though they do happen. But what I want you to understand is that those miracle stories don't matter, because you don't *need* an instantaneous shift in order to get life-changing outcomes.

From £420k to seven-figure entrepreneur in just 12 months

Would you like to hear a story about a quantum shift, anyway? Who wouldn't, right? OK, so in 2020, the year that everything stopped – remember that little thing called a worldwide pandemic? – I, in fact, tripled my annual turnover, growing from £420k in revenue to £1.2 million. I know. In the year that the whole world was spinning its wheels, how the hell did that happen? It really didn't make any sense to the outside world. While I certainly had an advantage, being an online business owner, this type of growth wasn't typical for all online business and mindset coaches at the time, at all. So, what was it about me at that time? My story was different because I became an energetic match for creating a seven-figure business. Whilst the actual transformation – the result – took place at the end of 2020, the quantum shift took place in 2019, when I was at a retreat in Colombia.

This retreat literally changed my life. I'd signed up because of the promise of being able to rub shoulders with other seven- and even eight-figure entrepreneurs. I already knew that the environment we put ourselves in can make a huge difference in how we feel, how we think, and how we see ourselves. I also know that when we put ourselves in an unusual environment, it can sometimes be easier to take new ideas, concepts, and possibilities on board, as full immersion in something new disrupts our usual ways of thinking. This is why I love to host and facilitate my own Infinite Receiving retreats.

When I got to Colombia, what I was most struck by was that the host of the event, Ron Reich, had gathered together a range of entrepreneurs who had all made their money in different ways. This was the first light-bulb moment. What it meant was, there was no *one* specific way to make money, there were a multitude of different ways. I just needed to find a way that worked *for me*. This was a win. It busted a myth that I was somehow 'missing the silver bullet,' the one specific strategy that all seven-figure entrepreneurs knew and that I didn't. A strategy that would be kept beyond my reach until I did know. The second big thing to strike me was how similar we all were. When I talked with many of the attendees on a human level, they talked about their kids, their partners, their wins and their challenges, their mindset blocks, their missions in the world... and I just kept thinking, 'I think like they think. I'm experiencing what they are experiencing... and if they're just like me in life, what's stopping me from being what they are like in business?' Looking for the similarities instead of the differences helped me to bust the myth that the reason that I couldn't do it was because I was too different. And with that I realised that I could become a seven-figure entrepreneur.

The seed had been well and truly planted, but that wasn't the end of it.

Now, when it comes to water, unless it's the Pacific Ocean in the middle of somewhere like Mexico and feels like a bath, I'm just not that into it. It plays havoc with my hair, I hate being cold, and I'm not the strongest swimmer. It's just not that much fun for me. But during this retreat, we spent a night river rafting in rapids and camping out underneath the stars. Not really my thing, but I'm there because I want to do things differently and I want to see things differently, so when it's my turn to get into the dinghy I don't put up too much of a protest. I get dunked a couple of times, I get cold, but overall, it's not too bad. I take my turn and think nothing more of things until the party seems to have slowed and has gathered round the base of a cliff. Everyone is looking up at it. I immediately think, *No way. This is not happening.*

The problem was, I had a team of people I'd been rafting with. One of them, Glen Ledwell, happens to be co-founder of Mind Movies (coincidently one of the first programs I had ever bought when I first started out in entrepreneurship), an electronic vision board that you can add music to – super cool. Now, Glen is an ultra-competitive, loud, and direct Aussie. So, after I vocalized the thought, 'There's no freaking way I'm jumping off the top of that cliff,' the response I got was, in no uncertain terms, 'Yes, you are.' And what happened was a couple of things: First, I was suddenly faced with the potential shame of letting down my comrades – this jump was no longer just about me; it was about our 'A-Team,' as Glen had named us. And second, it was also about whether I was willing to allow my fear to dictate my movements.

I decided to lie to myself. Not consciously, but lie I did. I convinced myself that I was just going to walk to the top of the cliff and if I didn't want to jump, then I would just walk back down. This was a ridiculous notion. There was only one way down from that cliff and that was jumping, but at that point, I wasn't ready to admit to myself that I was going to jump, so I just thought about the next step.

I see so many people stalling when it comes to creating their dreams and their desires, because they want to know exactly how they are going to get to the result, before they have even really started the race. The problem with life and business is that frequently, progress isn't linear, and trying to work out all the steps that are going to be needed when you are about to embark on something that you have never done before slows most people down unnecessarily. You're never going to anticipate all the steps – even with the best-thought-out plans. Sometimes, the only thing to do is to be willing to do whatever it takes – to take the next step, knowing that when the time comes, you'll be able to work out the subsequent steps from there.

So… I climbed to the top of the cliff and, just like in a Disney cartoon, I took a deep breath, raised my knees, and time appeared to slow down as I began running toward the edge. Beneath me, I heard not just my teammates but the entire group of participants counting me down: 'THREE... TWO... ONE....' As I got to the edge, my whole body froze in a comedic stop. Every cell in my body was screaming, 'No, what the hell are you thinking? There's no way you can go over the edge of this cliff!'

'But s***, there's no other way down.'

Before I – or anyone else – knew it, I took a couple of steps backwards for a much shorter run-up and I threw myself off the edge and the sound that left my mouth – I screamed so loudly – is something I'll always remember. It was like everything happened in slow motion while simultaneously being speeded up. My hand instinctively went up to hold my nose and my feet hit the water. And then my ankles, calves, thighs, body, the lot – until I was completely submerged. Automatically, my ankles began paddling furiously, and as my head once again broke through the surface of the water, I heard a deafening roar from everyone watching.

That jump was one of the most exhilarating, incredible feelings that I've ever experienced. As I slowly descended beneath the water and burst up through its surface – at that moment – I smashed through something else.

I had done it. And in that moment, what they'd witnessed was the making of a millionaire.

I had decided, without a doubt, that I was a match for seven figures.

Even though that was a very literal example of making a quantum leap, don't worry – you don't need to jump off a real-life cliff, abseil down a mountain, or take up parkour in order to make a shift. But what I realized on reflection was a shift in my consciousness and, ultimately, in my identity over the course of the retreat, that set me up, in 2020, for the wildest year ever in my career. That jump compounded the shift that had already happened while talking to those multi-millionaires on a physical level.

So, what exactly happened?

1. I changed my physical environment, which meant that for one whole week, my natural habits and patterns of thinking and living were completely interrupted. Changing your environment is helpful when you are looking to make a change because it makes it easier for you to take on new information and, in this case, new beliefs because you're surrounded by the new and the unfamiliar. Habitual thinking is created by seeing and thinking about the same things in the same way over and over again. So, when we interrupt the pattern, we create space for something new.

2. I was presented with evidence of other people's success. Multiple people all having achieved the result that I wanted and all doing it in their own way. This busted through any unconscious beliefs that I was having about needing to do things in a certain way. If they could do it their way, I could do it my way. There was no one right way to do it. Some people say you have to see it to believe it. While this isn't always true, in this case, the evidence that it was possible was overwhelming for me.

3. The more I chose to notice what was similar between the other entrepreneurs and me, the more my brain got on board

with it not just being possible to hit seven figures, but that it was possible for me.

4. In the jumping off the cliff, there was a cellular shift in my identity. I went from being the Black girl who doesn't really like getting her hair wet, not a massive fan of cold water, and who won't put herself in any crazy swimming situations that have the obvious potential for drowning, into the woman who's able to face her fears and jump off the side of a freaking mountain and survive (yes the cliff just became a mountain, because that was the size of the fear in my mind and in my body). And if I could do that, then I could do anything.

And I claimed in every cell of my being that in the next year, I'd be hitting seven figures. That's the story of my quantum shift, which over time became my quantum transformation.

Faith + Action = Miracles

This has been an affirmation that I've been using for over a decade. I started using it after reading the book *Think and Grow Rich* by Napoleon Hill. In that book, Hill tells the story of his unwavering belief that his son, who had been born deaf, would one day hear. And part of the strategy for turning that dream into a reality was to create positive expectation for the entire family through mantras and affirmations. This was inspiring to me, so when my son was born, I started speaking to him a nightly prayer that ended with the expression: Faith + Action = Miracles. While the prayer in its entirety didn't stick, this final phrase did, and I can honestly say it has changed my life. And if I were to break down the

Faith + Action = Miracles equation, my experience in Colombia was the equation in action. The retreat helped me tap into the faith part – the self-belief that a seven-figure income was possible. But of course, this was just the first step. It's what happened after the retreat that shifted my income from a dream into reality.

Following that retreat, I chose to hold on to the knowing that 2020 was going to be the year I became a seven-figure entrepreneur. From that point, I made big, bold money moves and I acted in alignment with that knowing. All the decisions I made in my business came from the standpoint of knowing that the following year was going to be the year that I made a million. I behaved like a millionaire. I hired the team that I needed to support me, I created products and services I needed to sell, I hired mentors to provide me with ongoing support as I changed the heart of my business. I set everything up to support the 'inner knowing' that things were changing for me. And it was freaking scary at times, but every action came from this place of knowing. Not proving, not hoping or wishing, but knowing what it was I was creating.

And it was from this place the miracle of tripling my turnover to £1.2 million happened.

Unfortunately, we can't all go to Colombia for a retreat to experience a dissolution of all our beliefs in a moment, but I want you to know that it doesn't matter, and you don't have to. While I take time out every year to put myself in new and different environments to accelerate my learning and evolution, what I'm absolutely clear on, and I've seen it most precisely and profoundly within myself and the people who I've worked with over the last 10 years, is that it's the compound effect of making small shifts every day in how you think, how you choose to feel, and how you choose to behave, when done consistently, that will change your entire life.

The one-degree shift

I'm sure you've heard it said before that when a pilot is flying a plane, the entire destination would change if they were just one degree out of sync with their flight map. Think of yourself as the pilot of your life and when you're not conscious of the one-degree shift, this is not a good a thing. But when you are consciously choosing to elevate what you are doing, how you are thinking and behaving, by just one degree every single day, within 12 months, you can change your entire trajectory. And your willingness to commit to this is what will create extraordinary results for you when it comes to amplifying your receiving across every area of your life. How do I know? Because this is what I live and experience every single day for myself, and this is what I teach my clients in The Infinite Receiving Portal program.

Can you imagine how things might change if you were able to make a one-degree shift in how you feel about yourself being a wealthy individual? Or a one-degree shift in awareness regarding who you believe yourself to be when it comes to finding the love of your life to 'I am a lovable individual; I'm an amazing partner'? Over the course of 365 days, those consistent one-degree shifts can change your entire life.

And of course, when you combine consistent one-degree shifts with a retreat or time spent in different environments with people who get you and where crazy things are happening, what do you think then happens? Your own quantum transformation unfolding over time.

So, when it comes to Infinite Receiving and creating the conscious wealthy life that you desire, it starts with the decision and then the awareness to work on your identity rather than focusing on the results. Inside out as opposed to outside in.

Are you ready?

There came a point in my life where I asked the question: 'What is it that you desire?' First, I started dreaming. Then I started claiming. Then I started living. Infinite Receiving is waiting for you.

~ Q&A ~

Q: *Is it possible to be happy with what you have and to still have big goals at the same time?*

A: Absolutely!

If you're setting a new goal because you feel like what you currently have isn't enough, then you're missing the point. True satisfaction comes from realizing that you are already whole, complete, and enough and in knowing how to feel safe within yourself. When you have this as a baseline, you are literally creating from a place of abundance. So, whatever you choose to aim for isn't driven by a sense of lack, but rather, a sense of curiosity. You wonder what else you can create and how much more you can allow yourself to receive, without needing external things to prove your worthiness or value – which has a whole different vibe to it. You can reach this place by doing the work in all three areas of the Wealth Trifecta: intrinsic, experiential, and leverageable wealth.

Remember: Growth and evolution are a natural part of our design as humans. So, why would we ever want to stop that amazing process? Whether it's making a bigger impact, nurturing stronger relationships, finding deeper purpose, or experiencing financial growth – all of it is good, and all gets to be fully embraced. So, keep growing, keep evolving, and keep welcoming all the wonderful things coming your way!

Faith + Action = Miracles

Chapter 4

Intrinsic Wealth and Self-Worth - the Connection

In the previous chapter we talked about the three different kinds of wealth – intrinsic wealth, experiential wealth, and leverageable wealth. And we discussed how, in order to expand your wealth across all areas of your life, you need to start with an identity shift. We worked on shifting our inner experience in order to change our outer reality. In this chapter we're going deeper into the 'how' you do this.

When it comes to receiving more and creating more wealth in our lives, our capacity to receive is often hindered by how much we truly value ourselves. It's common for many people I coach to have a low sense of self-worth when they embark on this journey. And it's important to understand that the level at which we perceive our own value directly impacts our progress. Even when a person appears super-confident on the outside, if their desire to create more has been formed from a foundation of not feeling enough, the conversation always circles back to them not feeling worthy or deserving enough to receive their desires.

When it comes to worth, it's useful to look at things in a similar way as with wealth:

- **Self-worth** (how we perceive our value)

- **Net worth** (how much we've accumulated)

- **External worth** (the value that we bring and is recognized by the world)

In my experience, what's true for wealth is also true for worth. Like with the Wealth Trifecta, the elements that make up the Worth Trifecta aren't actually linked. You can have people with high self-worth and low net worth, and with high net worth and very low self-worth. I've discovered through my clients doing this work, though, that magic can happen if you work on your self-worth alongside your net worth. But people usually want to focus

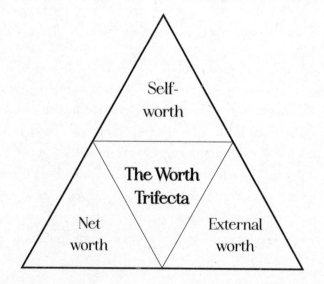

on their external worth first. The problem is that increasing your bank account, the number of cars you have, or the luxury holidays you go on will never help you increase your self-worth over time.

Getting more stuff will never make you value or love yourself more. Neither will focusing your attention on external value – seeking validation by people-pleasing or over-giving will not leave you feeling better about yourself. In many cases, you feel worse, as you deplete yourself and end up with a sense of being taking advantage of or like a victim of your circumstances, because everyone else's needs always come first.

As you step into the identity of a conscious and wealthy human being, you get to readjust the relationship between self-, net, and external value. You understand that your net value and your external value will never be able to increase your sense of self-value and, therefore, help you to create a life that you love. To wake up feeling happy and joyful, you don't need net worth or external value. Don't get me wrong, these two areas are important, but the foundation for the type of success that I'm talking about always starts with our self-worth and how we value our sense of self.

You don't have to look very far into the world of celebrity to know that this is true. As we touched on in the introduction to this book, we've all read or heard about people who, on the outside, appear to have it all: the cars, the homes, the luxury lifestyle, sometimes thousands or even millions of people who adore them and yet, on the inside, these stars feel broken, empty, and confused as to why, when they have everything that most people could ever dream of, they still feel like they aren't enough. Or less than they should be.

You can't use external factors
to fix internal problems.

What is self-worth?

When it comes to understanding self-worth, I often find myself reflecting on the wonderful world of babies. Just think about it for a moment: Does a little baby have to start walking before we see them as worthy? Do they need to utter their first words before we acknowledge their worthiness? What exactly must a baby do to be considered worthy? It's an intriguing thought, right?

Here's the thing: A baby doesn't have to do anything to be considered worthy. In fact, every baby is inherently worthy just by existing. The mere fact that they are here is the miracle.

Do you ever wonder why you're not living to your fullest potential? It's because you have forgotten that *you* are that miracle baby. In the previous chapter, we explored the idea that you're a multidimensional being with the ability to access the past while existing in the present. That same principle also applies here. My desire for you is that you remember that, like that baby, you too are inherently worthy just because you exist. You are a miracle, and nothing can add to your self-worth. It's innate and it's intrinsic. You were born 100 percent worthy.

Over time, your learned experience may have chipped away at your inner knowing. It's probably happened in multiple ways, both subtly and overtly. So, in part, the commitment to being a conscious wealthy human being is choosing to remember your worth every day.

Transformational Tools

Right now, I'd like you to write in your journal:

- What would I choose for myself if I knew that I was worthy?

- What would I choose for myself if I knew that I was deserving?

- How would I show up differently TODAY if I knew my life was worthy?

Notice how you feel while writing your answers.

Maybe you'll be uncomfortable asking yourself these questions, because, until now, you've been choosing based on what you need, or what is just good enough, i.e., 'It's not what I really want, but I don't need any more than this so it's OK.' And why is that? It's because you're not sure that you're good enough or that it's OK to say what it is that you truly desire. When so many other people make do with what they have, or just don't have the option for more, who the heck are you to say, 'more please'?

Remember the baby?

You're still that baby. You were worthy and deserving then and you're worthy and deserving now.

The journey to remembering our own worth rarely happens overnight. What has worked for me, as well as my clients, is to focus on small but consistent changes: wearing clothes that make me smile, because it's good to smile; breaking for lunch, because it's good for my mental and physical health; taking time to sit and meditate for five minutes in the morning, because I am worthy of starting my day in a peaceful way. So, rather than wanting or needing to wake up tomorrow feeling in every inch of your being that you're worthy and deserving of your dreams, hopes, and desires, focus instead on connecting with your worthiness, little by little, and choosing the one-degree shift in your awareness that impacts the way you think, speak, and know yourself.

Remember – just one degree every single day for the next 365 days. You can do more if you want to but commit to doing no less. Make that one-degree commitment to yourself today and begin your journey. And remember that the path may not be simple, but it will always be rewarding. My own journey of self-worth has been a long and winding one.

During my teenage years, I struggled with a low sense of self-worth, and it manifested in wildly promiscuous behavior. I was, as Abraham Hicks would say, 'looking for love in all the wrong places.' And because I didn't value who I was, I thought I could increase my sense of self and worth through external validation from other people.

Bad move.

There were a couple of incidents that shifted things for me over time. I've already touched on the first big one – when my mum passed away when I was 19 years old. The other pivotal shift for me came over a decade later, when I decided I didn't want to work in my corporate job anymore. It happened pretty much the moment I found out I was pregnant with Caesar, my eldest son. I distinctly remember thinking, *I want to be able to tell him he can do anything he wants to with his life*, and I wanted him to believe me, but as I looked around my life, I knew that I couldn't say that authentically and have him trust a single word that came out of my mouth. I had a job that I was good at, but that didn't light my soul on fire. It was just OK, and I had no desire to progress. I'd moved on from waiting tables, but essentially, I was still treading water.

While it took me getting pregnant again with Coco, my second child, to actually make the move, I did it. I thought, *If I don't do it now, I'll never do it.* You might be wondering, why did I think it was possible? And the truth is, I'd been building up my trust and capability muscles, by doing hard things. I had climbed the Atlas Mountains in Morocco, climbed to the top of the three biggest mountains in the UK, cycled to Amsterdam from London in 48 hours. I'd pushed myself and succeeded. If I could do those hard things, I could do this. So, when Coco was just a month old, I went to my first hypnotherapy and psychotherapy diploma class and about halfway through this training, I also decided to become certified in hypnobirthing – and the rest, as they say, is history.

What felt scarier than leaving the job was moving back into the classroom. Up until going back, I had run a narrative that said I wasn't bright enough. 'I'm not academic. I can't study. I'll never get a certificate. I'm a dropout.' That was my story. I was very attached to that identity at the time, so the decision to retrain was a big one. For it to be worth the investment, I had to decide: 1) that there was more that I could do; and 2) I was worthy of receiving more. Now, I wasn't calling it receiving at that point, but that's what it was. A decision to create and receive more in my life.

This decision first came from the inside. I decided that it was safe for me to embody the identity of the student. And as I chose this for myself, my behavior shifted. And that shift has been permanent – I haven't stopped studying since.

I decided it was OK to become a student again before I had any evidence that it was going to work out in my favor. However, the 'Why' I had for trying, which was to inspire my children, was big enough for me to be willing to make the choice to go all in for myself.

In the quietest of moments, I had to believe that I, Suzy Ese Ashworth, was worthy enough to be an inspiring mother both for my children and (I realized on reflection) for me. And after I chose to believe that, I started to take actions in alignment with being an inspiring mother. And where I really shocked myself was, because of my commitment to showing up daily, I only went and finished top of the class! My internal dialogue was... 'WTAF? How the hell did that happen?' This decision increased the value in each corner of my Wealth Trifecta. I remembered more of my intrinsic wealth; it increased my experiential wealth; and it would ultimately increase my leverageable wealth.

Your dreams are YOU honoring your innate
and intrinsic blueprint and desire to create.

Separate your self-worth from your external value

One of the most challenging tasks you are going to undertake on this journey is separating your self-worth from your external value. This requires daily intention. What do I mean by this?

What the world is willing to pay for what you do has nothing to do with your own self-worth or intrinsic wealth (that is worthy and rich you feel on the inside). Remembering this is an important daily practice as it's easy to say, but challenging to believe. And it's something that I'm committed to working on, even if it's for my entire lifetime.

Despite this, it still takes work for me to realize that if someone says that they don't want to buy my offer, or that they don't value it at the same price at which I value it, it doesn't mean that I, as a person, am not valuable or worthy.

Your value as a human is what you were born with; it comes from within and it's not something that anyone else can give you or take away from you. Your net worth is not connected to your self-worth. Your self-worth is not connected to your external worth. And your external value (what you put out into the world) is not connected to your net worth. They are all separate, and when you really live in that knowledge it will create a whole lot of freedom for you.

This is the remembering; this is the start of a new equation:

Remembering + Unlearning + Rewiring = Life-changing results

Sitting alongside the remembering, we have the unlearning. So, as I mentioned above, as babies we understand that we're already worthy, and our expectations around our needs being met are high. Then if we're lucky, we get to hold on to this knowing until about the age of two, when it's no longer socially acceptable to think that the world revolves around us and our needs. And we begin to learn that in order to feel loved, accepted, and acceptable we need to start to adapt ourselves and our behavior. We do what we need to do to fit in with the community – which starts off with our family, then graduates to our school friends, then the workplace – or risk being rejected, which we're hard-wired against at a cellular level, because it's simply not safe to be cast out.

When we lived in tribal communities, it was literally life-threatening to be cast out. You were way more likely to be eaten by a mountain lion if you weren't sleeping with the rest of your crew, so you did what you needed to do to protect your life. And while we're no longer at risk of being eaten by wild beasts in most parts of the world, it can still feel life-threatening to go against what our parents or our peers want for us. And so, often we compromise ourselves as we learn to 'play a game' that doesn't honor the truth of who we are. For many people, the denial of their truth will last a lifetime; and for others, they decide that a lifetime of denial is too much of a price to pay for their freedom and they start the unlearning process. Unlearning all the ways they have been taught to trade in their authenticity and integrity to please other people.

And this can feel wildly intimidating. Like when you start choosing to say no when you really mean no. Or, 'Yes, I'd love that' instead of, 'Oh no, it doesn't matter, I'm OK.' Honoring your ability to say no or yes might feel seem like a small thing, but it's pivotal when fully embracing and occupying your own space in an authentic way. Try it – it's radical.

And the rest of this book is also radical when it comes to unlearning and letting go of the things you refuse to put up with any longer. You'll increase your capacity to receive infinitely just by embracing and being your true self. What a trip!

The journey that we're on

As you commit to this journey, you're likely to run into a few common themes that my clients often face:

Feeling guilty about wanting too much

Frequently, especially when it comes to money, some people feel bad saying they want more. As if money in and of itself is a bad thing. It feels unsafe simply to want more, let alone have it. It's not a bad thing, it's just money. It's neutral. It's what you choose to do with money that will determine the impact of it on your life. And, as with everything else, there are those who make bad decisions with money, and those who make good decisions, irrespective of whether you consider them good or bad people.

Feeling fearful about losing it all

Those who have a high net worth and external value, the multiple six-figure and seven-figure earners that I meet daily, also express how having money can make them feel scared. They fear they're not going to be able to sustain it, that they might lose it, that people are judging them. That they aren't going to be able to repeat their success. It feels unsafe to have money.

Fear that it will never be quite enough

Some people on the path to receiving more money will say – even when they're receiving what might, to some, feel like a fortune – that it's only when they receive the next [fill in the blank] amount that they'll feel safe and happy.

These fears show up in this way because people aren't working on the Worth Trifecta and are continuing to entangle self-worth, net worth, and the external value they have to offer into the world.

I've learned from being in business that as soon as I start to worry about people thinking I'm a bad person if I receive a certain amount, my receiving will slow down. If I'm worried that someone is going to judge me or I'm going to make bad choices, I'll also slow down the flow of abundance. When I choose to acknowledge that I am an inherently good person who will for sure make mistakes in my life and mistakes with money, but that's just part of being a human being, living a full human experience, my peace with that knowing creates the expansion required for me to attract more.

Your ability to detach your self-worth from your net value will open your capacity to receive infinitely.

Transformational Tools

I'd love for you to finish the following sentence:

Asking for more feels_____.

If your answers include words like 'greedy, grabby, wrong, needy, awkward, shameful, tight, uncomfortable,' then you know that you have work to do here, and asking yourself little questions like 'Is this actually true?' or 'Is this always true?' can create some room for an alternative belief that you can start focusing your attention on.

If you wrote, 'exciting, juicy, beautiful,' then I invite you to explore whether that extends to every area of your life or just to certain areas? Where in your life doesn't it feel juicy and exciting?

If asking for more feels awkward to you, or you experience any of the challenging emotions listed above, what do you do with those feelings when you feel them?

Feeling safe and your nervous system

When it comes to expanding your own personal wealth blueprint, your number-one focus is feeling safe in the body. In fact, feeling safe is a requirement whenever you are looking to create change and transformation in your life. Feeling safe and feeling safe to feel. Most people are unaware that part of what's restricting their growth is their unwillingness to deal with the feelings of discomfort that they experience when they decide that they're both willing and ready to do things differently. In fact, often we decide that feelings of 'dis-ease' and discomfort are to be avoided at all costs. Why? Because we hate feeling uncomfortable and we don't want anyone else to feel uncomfortable.

Getting comfortable with the dis-ease that comes from being willing to look your fears in the face and still being able to tap into the frequency of safety is a crucial part of transforming your life. Even when the decision or commitment you're about to make feels scary or outrageous. I've often found myself in situations where taking action seemed intimidating, even reckless and irresponsible. But I still acted. While this courageous mindset is not the right path for everyone, the reason I was able to move in this way is because I understood how to feel safe in my body, even when the decisions or actions I was taking felt wild. I have noticed that people who are living lives that truly light them up in positive ways all seem to have this ability to access intrinsic safety.

Sounds like a lot of effort, right? It is. Because every experience that you've had, both positive and negative, leaves a mark – an imprint or a memory – in your body's nervous system. When we experience something negative, that imprint will resonate with the frequency of a wound. And what we do, consciously and subconsciously, is protect the wound from being touched again to avoid feeling pain. We control our circumstances, so we don't get triggered, so we don't feel uncomfortable, so we don't feel 'Not Good Enough.'

Some people have major traumas in their pasts, while others seem to have sailed through their lives with very few hiccups. But – trust me – everyone carries some things from the past that make it feel unsafe for them to boldly step forward, unsafe for them to really own their desires, and unsafe for them to say: 'This is really who I am.'

Now we have this awareness, we can help the nervous system by working *with* the wounds and working with the feelings that accompany those wounds, so that they're able to move through the body instead of remaining stagnant and stuck, and becoming the source of triggers.

It's about repairing – helping your nervous system to be as calm and peaceful as possible and knowing that you are safe, lovable, and worthy no matter what, in every situation regardless of what it is, as frequently as you can. Part of the reason that I'm able to feel safe, even when my mouth is clammy, my hands are dry, armpits sweaty, is because of the tools that I am about to share with you. They help me to feel my feelings, so that I can feel bad or embarrassed without it meaning something about my intrinsic value (or lack thereof). By choosing to operate from a place of fullness, I am able to focus on the knowledge that I am whole and complete, and enough, regardless of my external circumstances. This means that *I* am dictating my sense of safety, rather than my clients, money, or what other people are saying about me.

What I've realized on my journey to understanding
the person who feels wealthy in all areas is

that the more I allow myself to feel, the richer
I have become both emotionally and practically.

Feeling your feelings

So now we know that a huge and important element in increasing our capacity to receive wealth is being willing to feel our feelings. For some of you this may feel liberating and exciting; for others it may feel scary – and that's OK. Sometimes this is a cultural thing – hello to the Brits with their stiff upper lip and 'keep calm and carry on' attitude – but also this is huge in the personal development world when it comes to the interpretation of many of the manifestation teachings. Why? Because we're told negative feelings aren't allowed; that it's just not acceptable to feel angry, sad, or frustrated if you want to create the life of your dreams. So, when the negative feelings inevitably arise (because we are human beings who are experiencing the full 360 degrees of life) many of us shoot them down, hide, or bury them. Or we may fear acknowledging any 'negative' feelings about a thing in case it becomes too overwhelming – we're scared our feelings may just swallow us whole. If you recognize yourself in any of these scenarios, you're not alone. However, staying in this place will hinder your mission when it comes to receiving more in a way that is continual and sustainable.

I want you to understand that not only is it OK to feel what you feel and safe to feel all your feelings, but also to know that when you don't, those feelings don't go away. They actually stay with you, buried deep within the cells of your body. It's a bit like having your own secret lock box that you keep hidden away from prying eyes – I mean, just imagine the horror if cousin Tracy saw you losing your shizzle at your niece's party! That would never do – so we hide our feelings in our lock boxes to maintain a 'good' public face. But beyond shielding ourselves from curious onlookers, often it feels like self-preservation for us.

We're keeping our feelings locked away from ourselves. The problem with that strategy is twofold. First, that lock box isn't airtight. What I mean by that is every time you stuff a feeling into that box, it damages the integrity of the container, creating little holes for your feelings to trickle out. You might notice this in your body as underlying feelings of dissatisfaction or a general feeling of dis-ease that you're not quite able to put your finger on. Or maybe you feel easily activated by things that, on reflection, you're not sure why you have just lost your temper or got frustrated about, but there it is.

What's going on? Unresolved feelings and emotions are trying to make their way to the surface in order to be seen, acknowledged, listened to, or transmuted into something that is going to be more helpful to us once the lesson has been received. Our emotions always teach us something.

The second issue is the amount of energy that is required to keep all the emotions and the lock box sealed tight and buried. It's literally draining your life force. All the energy you're using to keep these parts of yourself hidden and contained stops you from being the creative person you were born to be; stops people from being able to see the fullness of who you are – and I'm not talking about them reveling in your negativity, I'm talking about what's left on the other side of you releasing those pent-up emotions.

Not only are other people being denied that version of you, but so are you. And it's the part of you that's on the other side of those feelings that, when allowed to see the light of day, is both your most magnetic and potent self when it comes to creating your desires.

Some people will call this healing, but I hesitate to use that word, because it creates the idea that something is broken within you and needs to be fixed. I don't believe that this is the case for anyone. What has been true for me, and for my clients, is when we drop the idea of needing to fix ourselves and focus on what it means to allow all parts of self to be present in our life, we experience a sense of integration, a feeling of fullness. We become 'full of ourselves,' free from the false beliefs that we're 'not good enough' or that we're 'broken.' And it's from this place of wholeness that we have a different experience of wealth across all areas of our lives.

It feels important to say that you also don't want or need to make this into a journey to Destination Wholeness, with you deciding that, until you get to that place, you're still not going to be worthy of receiving more. That would be swapping the luxury holiday for spiritual enlightenment and deciding that you're only worthy when... again. Same old shizzle, different packaging. Nope, we're not playing that game here. This game is about being willing to acknowledge and welcome all parts of yourself and, every time you forget and start to doubt the knowing that you are full, whole, and complete – even with every perceived imperfection that is yours – seeing how quickly you can come back to remembering that you are that baby. Yes. Even now.

The more frequently you can feel, release, and then come back to the center of that knowing, the more time you spend in the energy of creation, expansion, and receiving. This is the game.

What I'm really talking about is being willing to create a more sensational life. Moving away from numbing out, using distraction or avoidance to help create a more seemingly acceptable version of who you are. Alongside trusting that it's ok for a person to feel sad when something sad happens, and feeling sad doesn't mean that it's not possible to create and receive.

When I separated from my husband, I went through one of the saddest times of my adult life. I also knew that, more than ever, if I was going to be the mother I wanted to be for my children and be able to support our needs as a family financially, hiding from my feelings wasn't going to be the thing that would support us in a healthy or sustainable way. And it was through the understanding and applying of what I'm sharing here that, not only was I able to hold the feelings and emotions of my family during this tough time, but I was able to feel and allow my own feelings of grief, loss, and sadness, while still being able to create and receive more in my business than I had ever done before.

Can we feel fear and not let it consume us or stop us from moving forward? Can we feel shame and not make it mean that we're bad humans and therefore don't deserve to have hopes, wishes, and desires? The answer is yes. When you are willing to allow all parts of you to exist without judgment, when you are willing to allow all parts of you to have a voice and hear your own needs, while choosing to know that you are still worthy and deserving – it's from this place that it's still possible to receive.

I don't need to hide from myself or others, I don't need to fight myself or others, I don't need to deny myself or go into people-pleasing for others. Can you imagine how things might change if you began to lean into and live in this place of knowing consistently? I can!

Your job as a conscious, wealthy individual is to make the decision that you are capable of feeling all your emotions. You are the type of person who's willing to feel their emotions. You are the type of person who's willing to learn from their emotions. And, in the feeling, learning from, and channeling of your emotions appropriately, you are opening yourself up to receiving and integrating all of yourself.

I am becoming more full of myself and
as I become more full of all of myself,
I increase my capacity to receive.

E in Motion Tool

While people will often use the word release, it's not strictly accurate most of the time, because it implies that you are able to rid yourself of something. But science tells us that energy can't be created or destroyed, only transmuted, transformed into another form or type of energy. So, when you think about your emotions, rather than trying to 'rid' yourself of the ones that feel less comfortable, it's much more helpful to think of that energy being transformed.

What's also true is that when people are fearful about getting overwhelmed by their emotions, it's not the emotion itself that is creating the overwhelm. It's the meaning or the story that is present when you feel the emotion. So, learning how to separate the story or the meaning that is attached to the emotion, and how to focus solely on the feeling itself, plays a huge role in transmuting energy. The easiest way to do this is to become aware the moment you start questioning why, or explaining why you are feeling what you are feeling. Whenever you do this, you're giving the feeling a storyline; you're *thinking* about the feeling instead of *feeling* your feelings – and it's in the thinking about the feeling a person will often get trapped.

Through my own studies, I was introduced to a practice by Inner Voice Facilitator Bella Lively, and the practice below is a variation on one of her tools. I call this the *E in Motion Tool.* The E stands for both energy and emotion. Our emotions are just energy in motion and function solely to signpost things that have or need our attention. When they get stuck within the body, it's because it doesn't feel safe for us to keep the flow of energy moving. Whether this happens consciously or not, it creates problems for us that can manifest in the way that we feel emotionally and physically, while also impeding what we feel it's possible for us to receive. So, with this simple tool, I'm going to share with you how you can stop holding onto stagnant energy and create space and expansion within yourself, so you're no longer slowing down your pace of receiving by holding onto energy that is no longer serving you.

Disclaimer – When tuning into old stories, feelings, and emotions, the most important thing to consider as you embark on your journey of transformation is to go only as far as feels safe for you in the moment. You get to take radical responsibility for your own well-being at all times, so if the idea of revisiting a certain emotion feels unsafe for you in the moment, don't push yourself further than where it feels appropriate for you in this given moment. Knowing that all the tools outlined in the book are designed for you to use repeatedly over time, nothing needs to be forced or rushed. So always go at a pace that feels right and appropriate for you.

You'll find an audio version of the *E in Motion Tool* in the *Empower You Unlimited Audio* app (search 'Meditations for Infinite Receiving'). Or, if you prefer, you can record it in your own voice and play it back.

Transformational Tools

Set a clear intention to allow any energy that is no longer serving you to move through the body and be transmuted into the energy of peace and safety for the highest good of yourself and anyone you meet.

For this exercise we're going to be using the wisdom of the heart and your breath - tools that you have within you all the time. Our heart space contains wisdom and knowledge that goes beyond the logical thinking of the brain, which we will talk about later in the book. But for this exercise, I invite you to just follow the instructions outlined and notice how your heart energy is already able to guide you.

Step 1: Be in a seated position - ideally - and close your eyes. In a space where you have privacy and can make noise if you desire.

Step 2: Breathe in through the nose and out through the mouth as many times as you need to feel your body relaxing.

Step 3: While you don't need to count your breath, allow your exhalation to be almost twice as long as your inhalation.

Step 4: As you feel your body beginning to let go, bring your awareness to the top of your head and scan yourself from top to bottom, noticing anywhere where your energy feels dense or heavy.

Step 5: If you have found more than one area that feels tight or heavy, tune in to your heart space and ask your heart, which area is the priority right now?

Step 6: Ask your heart, is there emotion that is ready and wanting to be released right now?

Step 7: If the answer is no, give yourself permission to remain seated with your eyes closed, breathing in through your nose and out through your mouth for as long as feels comfortable for you, before ending your session.

Step 8: If the answer is yes, tune in to the part of the body where the emotion is living without adding any meaning or any story to the feeling. This is very important. The moment you find yourself thinking about what it is you are feeling, instead of just feeling, first bring your attention back to the breath and, once your thoughts have passed, tune back into the feeling.

Step 9: If the feeling were a shape, what shape would the feeling be? It might be a circle, a triangle, a basketball, a tractor. Just intuitively notice what shape the emotion is. Continue feeling the feeling and breathing.

Step 10: If the shape had a color what color would it be? Continue feeling the feeling and breathing.

Step 11: Allow yourself to keep feeling the emotion, and with every exhalation, notice how the shape gets smaller and the color fades.

This might take 2 minutes, 10 minutes, or half an hour. There's no set time, or number of breaths; you don't need to think about anything; your only job is to breathe and use the breath to release the emotion from the body.

As the emotion gets smaller, you might feel the urge to cry, or shout, or scream; you might want to move your body; you might desire to stand up, to shake, or stamp your feet. Or it might be a quiet and still experience except for the breath. All these things are completely normal. Just notice what the body desires to do and trust its wisdom, knowing that you only have to go as far as feels safe and comfortable for you.

After this energy has moved, you may feel tired, or drained; you might feel lighter or completely energized. All this is normal.

Step 12: When the shape gets to 10 percent or less than its original size, bring your awareness back to the heart space and tune in to a feeling of love. If that feels very easy for you to tap into - perfect. If this feels a little trickier, think of a person or a place that you love.

Step 13: Place your hand on your heart and imagine the feeling of love like a flame in your heart. Every time you inhale, notice the flame getting bigger and as you exhale, breathe the flame, the energy of love around your body. Do this for as long as it takes to fill the entire body with the frequency of love and, only when you are ready, to complete the exercise, bring your attention back to the center of your heart space and open your eyes, coming back fully present. To the here and now.

Well done. You have just released or transmuted old stagnant energy and filled the space with love, which is not only the number-one agent for transformation, but the most potent foundation for consciously creating what it is you desire.

I invite you to use this exercise daily. After I became very familiar with it, I'd even do mini sessions as I was walking along the street, when I'd notice fear or shame that was present in my body. It was liberating to be willing to feel what I was feeling without fear, as well as also being able to not feel the need to hold on to the emotion.

Be mindful, this exercise isn't solely about letting go, it's about being willing to feel, without compounding how we feel by adding story and meaning that keep the feelings locked in place. The power is in the feeling and then ultimately creating space for love. Filling yourself with love that you have created and allowed into your inner world. Did I already say this is where the magic starts to happen?

If you are a divine expression of Source, you can't be any better than who you are right now at your core.

~ Q&A ~

Q: I was feeling aligned and happy the last few days, but this morning my ex-husband sent me a message that really triggered me. I work full time in an office as I'm building my business on the side, and I can't take the time to really feel my emotions and shift out of this. I feel blocked and tense, which doesn't serve me. What do you do in cases like this?

A: I totally get it! It's amazing how we can be feeling great and in sync with ourselves, and then someone comes along and pushes all the wrong buttons. It's like a sudden jolt that throws us off balance. And these circumstances are challenging because you want to clear the difficult emotions immediately, and you don't feel you have the space for it.

So, one of the most exciting things that you get to learn and to master is, 'How do I sit in the void? How do I sit in the discomfort?'

Can you get to a place where you can observe the frustration and identify where you feel it most in the body, while recognizing that it doesn't have to overwhelm all of you? Can you get to a place where you are able to experience the feeling and not have that completely hijack your mind? Knowing that it's only a small part of you that feels frustrated, can you be open to experiencing other, higher vibrational emotions that will serve you more in the moment until you have the time and space to process what has been activated by your ex-husband? Is that possible?

Absolutely. Does it take time and intention? Yes, for most people, but it's possible. Making peace with just feeling a bit uncomfortable is the solution here. Growing your emotional intelligence to a space where you can experience all emotions without them hijacking you is the solution to this question in the first instance.

And then, it's like, 'OK, is it possible to create a world where I'm not triggered by my ex-husband's text?' Also, possible.

Faith + Action = Miracles

Chapter 5

Creating Wealth

In this chapter we're going to talk about consciously creating *exactly* what you desire, with an emphasis on financial wealth. So, let's not be coy. I'm going to dive straight in and start this chapter with a question. When it comes to money, what do you want? Please write the answer in your journal.

Often, when I ask this question of my clients, the first answer they give is something non-specific, like 'Lots!' Why would they do this? Mainly, it's out of fear. Fear of not hitting the number they have declared and then feeling bad or disappointed about it, or disappointed in themselves. This in turn re-ignites their fear of not being good enough. But this isn't you now, is it? Because you know how to feel your feelings and you're not playing the game of entangling your self-worth with your net worth. This isn't what we do around here… and if you were ambiguous with your numbers, there's no need to beat yourself up. This shows you where you get to notice, more quickly than ever, when you are still operating in alignment with the old story.

One powerful question to shift you out of the old space and into the new is: *If I wasn't afraid, what would I choose for myself?* What's your number? How much would you love to be earning a month, or a year? Pick whatever figure feels most fun for you to work with right now.

Now, while I've worked with mentors who share that they have never set themselves money goals because it's limiting, after experimenting with this myself and doing the work around separating net worth from self-worth, I've found that setting specific money intentions is the best form of focus and motivation for me. This isn't for the reason you might think, however. It's not actually about the money. Rather, it's about what the money represents.

If I hit my money goal, which is to someday be running a business that turns over £10 million a year, that means I've built a brand that is helping thousands and thousands of people around the world. That money represents a tidal wave of positive impact all around the globe and, at this stage in my life, it feels possible for me and exciting. And when I feel excited, it tells me that I'm right on the money (excuse the pun!)

I recommend picking a number that lights you up, a number that you're unlikely to hit in the next 30 days, 60 days, or even a year. Go for a number that feels stretchy and expansive. Sure, it might take you five or even ten years to reach your goal, but the timeline is irrelevant as the 'best' numbers aren't logical or linear. Your number doesn't have to make sense to the outside world, but it must make sense and feel good to you in your body. I'll share more about why later in this chapter.

While you may not always choose to work with money goals, for many people, it's helpful at the beginning of their money journey to work with something specific. If you really don't feel excited about making or receiving more money, however, think about the number of clients you want to work with instead. Or anything you desire to do that is going to require financial resources.

So, if you haven't already done so, please make a note in your journal and give yourself a number. What's the number that feels aligned for you right now? This is how much you want to be receiving – how does it feel? What do you notice when you write that number down? What are the emotions that you notice in your body?

This is your vision. Draw the letter V in the center of a large circle, with the number it represents next to it.

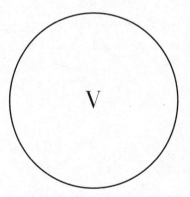

Now jot down how much you are earning right now. Notice how that feels. Notice if it's uncomfortable for you to write that figure down and next to that draw the letter R and put it in the center of a smaller circle. This is where you are right now.

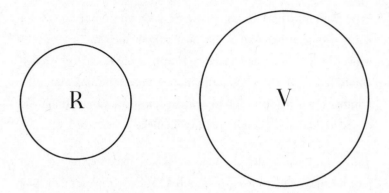

Now do the math – work out what the gap is between where you are right now and where you desire to be. Is it a 5k gap, 10k? 20k? More? Now you're clear on the gap, how does that feel?

Draw a line on the page from where you are to where you desire to be.

So, the next question is, what's stopping you from already being where you desire to be? This isn't a rhetorical question, by the way. I want you to write in your journal all the things that you feel are stopping you.

You might come up with things like:

- lack of skill set

- lack of support

- feeling overwhelmed

- lack of infrastructure

- feels like too much hard work

- unsure how to get to that point

Don't be shy, write down *all* the reasons you can think of. Then, on the line you have drawn between where you are and where you are going, I want you to draw a vertical line that represents each one of the things that are limiting you.

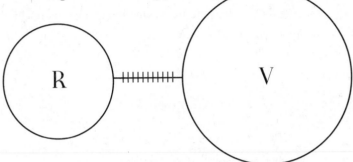

What I want to make clear before we go on, is that even though the vision you have for yourself is in a bigger circle, that circle isn't bigger because it's a bigger, better, shinier, more-accomplished version of you. That's really important to know.

Both circles are you as you are now. They are both you. The vision you have for yourself is placed in a bigger circle because it represents how much more of yourself you are willing to *become*. How much more space you are willing to take up. The vision you have for yourself is full of... yourself – in the best possible way!

Is your mind allowing that to be true? Can you allow that to be true for you?

If you answered 'no' to that question, add another vertical line to the gap between where you are and your vision. This line represents your doubt, and all these lines represent your limiting beliefs about your ability to create the money that you desire. All these beliefs ultimately show up as resistance and self-sabotage, and you'll see that not only in how you think, but in how you are willing to behave. On your Infinite Receiving journey, you'll need to remove or transform each of these beliefs, one by one, reducing the barriers and narrowing the gap between where you are and where you desire to be.

~ Affirmation ~

It's safe for me to honor my desires. It's safe for me to want and receive more.

Money goals in business

Let me ask you this: in terms of your financial goals, as you run your own business, how often do you look at the result that you want and then ask yourself, 'How do I get there? What do I need to do to get there? What's the process?'

These are good questions, but you'll get better and more consistent results if you ask, '*Who* do I need to be in order to receive this result?' Firstly, by focusing on the 'what', you work from the outside in, instead of from the inside out.

Using the outside-in system, you may see a little success, but it tends to be feast or famine. Sound familiar? 'I'm doing really well. Now everything is s***. Doing well again. Oh no, it's really s*** again.' It's a hokey-pokey style of financial success.

What's happening is that in order to get the result, you feel you need to push, to make it happen, and while this might work to a certain extent, because you haven't worked on who you need to be to hold, maintain, and grow your financial success, self-judgement kicks in, fear kicks in, doubt kicks back in. AND the negative associations you have with the feeling of pushing at all costs, such as doubting your worthiness, leave you feeling as though you're right back at the beginning. Sound familar?

Before we move on to how to remove your resistance, I want you to go back to your list of reasons you're not yet where you desire to be. Notice how many of the things that you wrote down were systems- and process-related, i.e. 'how' reasons: If I only knew how, then I'd be able to do it. Probably more than half, right? Of course, this is the most natural place for businesspeople (and most people) to go when they're looking to solve a problem. But that doesn't mean that it works. To see different results, you need to commit to seeing the world through a different lens and to focusing on the *who* rather than the *how* first.

This is one of the most challenging things you'll need to get your mind to play ball with you on, because we have a lifetime of conditioning that involves focusing on the result, rather than the identity of the type of person who gets the result.

What I find really interesting is a concept that you may hear from mindset and money mentors, such as my friend and first money mentor Denise Duffield-Thomas. It's called the 'new level old devil.' In essence, it explains how you can maintain doing well, but when it comes to growth and moving to your next level of receiving, the same old fears around being worthy of the next level, imposter syndrome, and fear of what it might take from you rear their ugly heads once more. You start the self-flagellation all over again: 'I should be doing this differently. I should feel better now. I should know better now.' And every time you use 'should' on yourself, you create more resistance.

The other form of fleeting success that I want to talk about is those times when you've worked hard for the launch or to cinch the deal, and you've got exactly what you thought you wanted, you've nailed it, and you feel great! You feel great for about five minutes and then you feel flat; you don't feel good at all. You've reached destination anticlimax, which hits even harder when you've been toiling away because of the story you told yourself: 'I'll feel better when it's done,' or 'Success will make me feel great about myself. I'll be worthy.' And let's not forget, 'I'll finally feel deserving when….' And while you might even feel great, worthy, and deserving for a short time, all the insecurities that were there before you did the thing are still there now you've finished it.

The other reason people feel that sense of flatness is that it's often only after the achievement that it occurs to you how much you've sacrificed in terms of your experiential wealth to get what you want. You quickly realize that no amount of money is worth sacrificing life and health for. When you get what you desire via this 'sacrificial' route, while it's totally possible to continue on that path for a lifetime, it's not possible to continue on that path and feel happy and joyful. If you ever read about Ebenezer Scrooge, you'll get the gist. Like Scrooge, who worked hard and accumulated wealth, many people find themselves missing out on true happiness and fulfillment despite their financial success. While that is an extreme fictional example, what tends to happen when people sacrifice their experiential wealth in the hope that leverageable wealth or net worth is going to make them feel better/good on the inside, is that the nervous system steps in and they begin to feel dis-ease at the way life is panning out. Slowly, but surely, external success or wealth starts to lose its appeal in the best-case scenario, and to feel unsettling and unsafe at worst. The true price of financial success becomes too high if you have chosen to sacrifice your experiential and intrinsic wealth.

Which is why people frequently move into the either/or space. It's money OR my happiness. It's work on my inner game first and then I'll be ready to receive more, and while the second half of this statement has more validity, as we saw on pp.36–7 in order to be truly wealthy, your willingness to work on all three areas of the Wealth Trifecta is where the magic – true wealth – really lies. So, the question then becomes, is it possible to work on all three areas of the Trifecta simultaneously? Absolutely!

The mission for you now is to commit to not only seeing things differently but doing things differently. And that doing starts with you being who you need to be. You get to start with 'who' when you're adopting the identity of a truly wealthy, conscious individual. And from the 'who', you then decide what conscious wealth gets to look like for you.

The 'who' begins with your core beliefs. What are core beliefs? They're the foundations for how we view the world, that ultimately determine what we expect to experience on a daily basis and, ultimately, over a lifetime.

Uncomfortable truth: Your continued willingness to bargain with what your soul desires is the only thing stopping you from getting the thing, doing the thing, and being the thing. STOP compromising!

Transformational Tools

Let's play a game. I want you to take the number that you chose when you wrote down your bigger vision, and I want you to multiply it by 100.

I want you to multiply it by 100 because what's interesting to me is that for many of you, your bigger visions are not far removed from what you think is possible. Which isn't the worst thing in the world, but when it comes to thinking about the different ways you get to start thinking about yourself, money, what's possible, and what you feel your current limitations are, multiplying your money goal by 100 puts you in a whole different stratosphere. Stick with me…

The next step is to write down all the reasons that your target multiplied by 100 is not possible for you. Write them all down. Don't overthink it - set the timer on your phone for five minutes and write down every reason that you *can't* achieve this number.

When I do this exercise with clients, typically I get answers like: I don't know how; this number is just way too big; no one needs that amount of money; I don't have the infrastructure; I don't have enough people in my audience; my customer service would collapse; I don't have the energy; that would take way too much work; people would judge me; how am I capable of creating that kind of a following?

What's interesting is when people look at the list of things they have written down, for many, there are way more things on the list that relate to not having the process, system, or strategy required to get the result they want. And every time I see this, I get people to pause and reconnect with what they know to be true when they're creating anything new in their lives. Yes, the system and process are important, but it's not the first thing that's stopping you. The biggest thing that will always put the brakes on you finding the solutions to all the problems that you think are going to come up lie in the realm of IDENTITY – who you are going to need to be and what you need to believe in order to give yourself the chance of expansion.

Look again at the list of barriers you wrote down. Are most of the perceived limitations *who* problems or *how* problems? If you went with 'how,' you're not alone. But this is where ensuring you put yourself in environments where people can reflect to you where you've slipped back into your old paradigm thinking is so helpful.

The second interesting truth is that everything you wrote down as a problem when you were thinking about receiving 100 times what you are receiving now is precisely what's slowing or preventing you from expanding into your actual goal right now.

For example, if you said, 'I don't have the right support to ×100 my wealth,' what you'll notice is that you are either doing too much in your business right now, or in order to make the leap to the next step, you know you're going to need to be willing to ask for more support in your life now.

If you wrote that you fear people judging you (which is an identity fear), there's also a part of you that fears being judged now – and that's the part of you who's scared to talk about money or even share your desire for more.

Everything you need to know about yourself now is written in your ×100 list.

This exercise is super helpful because it highlights that our natural tendency, even after all that you have read so far, is to go to the HOW of achieving, rather than the WHO of being, even when we intellectually agree and understand why the inner game is so important. So, the invitation is to keep remembering that the question always gets to start with, 'Who would I need to be to allow, create, or make _____?' You fill in the blank.

Now, I get it – 100 times your figure. Really? You don't need millions a year or tens of thousands a month. And the answer to that is, of course you don't 'need' it, but this conversation wasn't ever about working with what we need, it was about desire. And while you may not desire 100 times your original goal, by writing out your fears and concerns at that level, you also get to see what's keeping you from increasing your capacity to receive more of what you desire now.

It's also very useful for you to see just how easy it is to come back to operating from a place of need, which you must be willing to let go of if you are making the decision to step into your next level of wealth.

Fear is the thing that holds everyone back from their ultimate desires and their ultimate potential. In the past, I've been told that I need to eradicate my fears, but the more I've grown, the more I've realized that it's not about eradicating my fear – it's about learning how to dance with it.

Shedding the familiar

I want to remind you that you have committed to operating on a frequency of more, and this is where the rubber meets the road, because you get to choose, 'Do I want more, or don't I want it?' For most people, the answer is that they don't want more. Usually that's because they're operating from a place of fear, not wanting to be outside of the comfort, familiarity, and security of need. And there's no judgment from me about that.

People opt to operate in the space of wanting 'just enough' because it's familiar and safe, and because the idea of being different from friends and family, of outgrowing other people, feels scary. And this is why the three dimensions of wealth – intrinsic, experiential, and leverageable wealth – are so important, because when you notice that you're feeling afraid of outgrowing, when you notice that you're feeling afraid of receiving more because you're going to be operating in a completely different realm, that's when the intrinsic wealth element comes into play and the emotional work happens.

The reason we work on the elements of the Trifecta at the same time is so that you're capable of not just having five minutes in that bigger version of yourself where you're taking up more space, but so you can hold it, you can be it. You can allow wealth to flow through you, around you, and over you without feeling like you need to contain it yourself.

And by 'wealth' here, I mean so much more than just money. I mean that if you do this work, you'll start to experience the fullness of who you are and the richness of your life. Your money goals will become a tool to help you expand your field of awareness, increase your belief in what's possible for you, and encourage you to look and show up in the world differently. But, at the same time, you'll be able to let go of the idea that having more money will make you feel good about yourself. This is a game changer.

What do I mean by doing the work? Committing to a one-degree shift every day in your thinking, your feeling, and your doing when it comes to knowing that you are a whole, complete, and valuable human being – this is you doing the work. Choosing to expand into the knowing that it's safe for you to receive on a completely elevated level; this too is the work you have already started. If you need help, sign up for 365 days of daily prompts and affirmations with my one-degree-a-day reminders (p.235). Can you imagine what life gets to look like as you deepen your commitment to working on all three dimensions of your worth and wealth for a year? Just one degree a day, and your entire life gets to change.

One of the things I've noticed about myself over the years is that I'm really kind to myself; I choose to talk kindly to myself, I'm so generous to myself, and that's because of the work that I've done in the intrinsic wealth area. I'd be happy for my best friend to borrow the voice inside my head for a day. She would hear nice things about herself, encouragement, and cheerleading about the next step. This wasn't always the case though; I learned how to train this voice, so that it supported me rather than doubted me or held me back, and this has been a massive part of the intrinsic wealth piece. I have my own back, even when I mess up (which is frequently), and that makes everything else so much easier.

Forget all the reasons why it won't work and
choose to focus on the one reason it could.

Time and money

I'm keenly aware that among the things that cause stress when it comes to setting financial goals in your business are timelines, deadlines, and just time in general. We're obsessed with it. We need time to organize ourselves in the world – without it, life would be chaos. We need time to help us distinguish between the present moment and what we perceive as the past, even though there's an increasing amount of scientific evidence that there's only ever the present moment. The past and the future only exist in our minds.

This is helpful to consider when we're looking to release our attachment to the results of tomorrow, or who we're going to be tomorrow when the imaginary perfect circumstances to support our change miraculously present themselves. Spoiler alert: If tomorrow isn't happening, you don't need to wait to give yourself permission to be who you are evolving into today.

In Gay Hendricks' book *The Big Leap*, he describes a concept called Einstein Time where he shares examples of people being able to cover distances that shouldn't be possible by shifting their intention and the relationship they have with time. Almost as though they were able to slow time down in order to get to where they needed to get to in the perfect time.

Again, while this is all good in theory, what I've found to be the most useful tool for me in my own relationship with time and timelines is to set bigger, much bigger, goals than it is possible for me to hit in 30 days and frequently, even 365 days.

So, when I talk about creating a business that will eventually turn over £10 million a year, this isn't something that my brain has decided is possible for me to do next year, but it has decided that during my lifetime – which could be two years, five years, or literally a lifetime – that figure is possible for me. I know that in order to turn that intention from a goal into my reality, my job is to identify all my areas of resistance that stop me from being the type of person who could be turning over that amount of revenue in a year, and one by one remove the resistance bars and take the appropriate aligned actions in my business to make that happen. And, when I choose to know that everything is happening in the perfect time, which is only now, *and* simultaneously know that the perfect now might take me a lifetime, I'm doing a few things:

1. I'm removing the pressure. No fixed timelines means I've removed the stress.

2. I'm continually recommitting to the vision of the version of me that is doing it one degree a day – removing the timeline doesn't work if you forget your intention.

3. I'm observing and celebrating all the smaller milestones that I'm hitting on the way to the big intention.

4. I'm remembering that, for me, £10 million in turnover isn't actually a money goal, it's an impact goal. If I create a business that is turning over that much income, it means I'll be helping and supporting a huge number of people, and that is so freaking exciting to me.

Now, the other thing that's happening is that all the time I'm working on my leverageable wealth, my commitment to the other two realms means that it doesn't even matter whether I actually hit this number in my life or not. This number isn't needed for me to know my intrinsic value as a human. This number isn't needed to feed my family. This number won't make me better than anyone else.

The only thing it does for me is demonstrate how effective I am at aligning to my dreams and desires. That's it. And because of my commitment to my intrinsic and experiential experience of life and wealth when I dream big like this, while doing the inner work and ensuring that I'm still allowing myself to live life, I can view each of the steps I take on the journey to *becoming* as wonderful parts of a whole masterpiece. I get to enjoy the journey to the result. Bye-bye anticlimax, hello life that I'm loving!

And what's even more interesting is the more I allow myself to enjoy the learnings that happen in the moment, the less time things seem to take. It's a mind-bender, but a fun one.

The 'how' becomes so much easier when
you have got the 'who' nailed.

Transformational Tools

Look at the first money goal number you wrote down in your journal and then what you wrote when you multiplied that number by 100. Then, think of a number that represents a stretched intention that you can energetically get excited about. It might be the same as your original number or it might be bigger. Remember, you are not focusing on the timeline. This isn't something that you are shooting for over the next 30 days or even year. It's just at some point in the future that you feel you'll be aligned to this bigger number.

Now I invite you to create a future memory of how it gets to feel once you have received that money.

- What are the dominant emotions: joy, gratitude, peace?

- How do you feel in your body? A sense of safety or is it excitement?

- What's it going to mean to your family when you hit this number; how might it impact your wider community?

- Who's the first person you are going to share the news with?

- How will you celebrate?

Create as detailed a picture as possible. You can either write this down or imagine it in your mind's eye – whatever feels most aligned – but take the time to connect with this memory.

I also want you to think about how you might navigate any of the bumps on the journey to receiving this number.

- How will you show up when you're tired, but still in alignment with the bigger number?

- How will you choose to show up if you get hit with a curveball?

- How will you choose to show up if the plans that you made have to change suddenly at short notice?

You can also choose to look more specifically at any fears you might have about this next level and again anticipate how you are going to choose to respond to this moment, in alignment with the expanded version of receiving you have for yourself.

What's super helpful about doing this type of exercise is that the brain can't tell the difference between what's real and what's imagined, so if you take the time to keep connecting with the future memory in your mind, while allowing yourself to connect with the feelings of these moments – the feeling part is really important –

the mind as a problem-solving pattern machine literally starts to look for familiar or similar patterns to what you have created in your future memory experience. It will start to create scenarios, patterns, or experiences that lead you to the destination that you have already created in your mind's eye.

So, the key takeaways from this chapter are:

- Every time you feel stuck, notice if you are coming from *how* or *who*.

- Know you do not need to choose between your intrinsic wealth, your experiential wealth, and your leverageable wealth.

- Money and leverageable wealth are not bad and they will never be the things that will increase your sense of self-worth.

When you work on all three dimensions of the Wealth Trifecta, you open up a whole new level of receiving. Abundance flows through you and around you, you are choosing not to push or grab or force, and you give yourself permission to think bigger, asking for what you desire, not just what you need.

From this point on, you are leaning into your desires. Finally, say out loud, 'From this point onwards, as I build my wealth, I'm honoring my desires.'

Q1: *How do you stay focused when there's so much financial doom and gloom around at the moment? How do you move out of that energy?*

A: The same piece of advice has been echoed to me many times throughout the years, particularly from mindset and money mentors, but also in books – and that is in every recession there are winners and losers.

It's never all good. And it's never all bad. However, when your focus is occupied by people who are fearful and afraid, who are making decisions from a place of fear and projecting their fear into the future, naturally you start to feel anxious. It's true that if you are your own boss, there's a different level of agility that you have in comparison to someone on a fixed salary in a nine-to-five job. It's important that you recognize that and make sure you are mindful to be exercising confidence, courage, creativity, and agility when it comes to responding to your desires and ever-evolving world events.

Either way, use the tools in this book to stay centered, and look to surround yourself with spaces and with people who aren't scared, or in protective and defensive mode. Spaces like the Portal on my website.

I'm not a financial advisor, so it's important to seek professional advice if you're concerned about your financial well-being. What has served my clients and me the most, particularly during challenging economic times, is to be able to see alternatives.

Look for examples of what's possible and have those examples act as real-life tangible examples of other people's future memories turned into reality. Because as soon as we can see something is possible for someone else, it creates an opening for what's possible for us.

It's also important to pick your environments wisely. Notice if you're in places or environments where you are constantly feeling drained or pessimistic, and notice where you can limit your time in those spaces. Actively seek out people who are making positive moves to create the one-degree shift per day in their overall experience of life, both inside and outside of money.

And make sure you've done your homework on how the person who has what you desire chooses to navigate situations like this in a way that is in the highest good for everyone.

Q2: In your workshop, I've heard you say, 'I create my own reality.' What does that actually mean?

A: I think nowadays that phrase can feel like a controversial statement. So, to clarify, for me that doesn't mean I'm in control of everything in the universe. If there's a natural disaster, it's not because I've had a negative thought. However, if there's a natural disaster or anything that is objectively considered to be 'bad,' what I'm in control of is how I choose to respond in the moment. And how I choose to respond to 'whatever' experience that is in front of me is going to determine my experience of the next moment. Which then becomes my reality. I'm in control of the way that I respond.

Faith + Action = Miracles

Part II

Tools for Expanding Your Conscious Wealth

Chapter 6

Pillar of Infinite Greatness – You Are a Miracle

Now that we've delved deep into our understanding of wealth, it's time to uncover the precise steps we need to take to attract more abundance, infinitely, in every aspect of our lives. Let me introduce you to the 'Four Pillars' framework, starting with the Pillar of Infinite Greatness, where we'll amplify your Infinite Greatness codes. To invite greater prosperity into your life and business, it's essential for you to tap into your unique and infinite 'field of greatness.' As we do this, remember that our work always begins from the inside out.

I've learned, through my own ongoing transformational journey, that before we can make any meaningful changes we must begin with a clear understanding of where we're starting from. It's why I asked you to begin this journey by filling out the Wheel of Infinite Receiving on p.6. So, to begin the next leg of our journey together, let me ask you another question. (You know me – I'm a coach, and that's what we do!) When you reflect on your life and who you are in this moment, do you see yourself as great?

Most people fall into one of the following camps:

1. Duh... of course I'm great – let's go!
2. Umm... this feels a little egocentric. I mean, I'm good, but I'm not necessarily better than anyone else. I'm not special; this feels weird.

Which one most resonates with you? Write it down in your journal with the date next to it.

Now let me ask you a slightly different question. Would you love to be recognized for your unique greatness? I'm talking about people being able to see you and acknowledge your greatness, regardless of your job title, bank balance, or your professional and personal network. I mean, really being *seen* by others. Would you relish that?

As you're reading this book, I hope you answered 'yes' to this question! But even if you answered 'no,' that's OK, too. Because when you are ready to be and to feel seen, you'll know it. And hopefully, that will be by the end of this chapter.

In my years of working with clients, both in life coaching and in business, I've discovered something that's true for us all. Deep down, we all yearn to be seen and acknowledged. Some people desire recognition on a global scale and other people just wish their mum and dad would understand them and appreciate their unique qualities. There's nothing wrong with wanting to be seen. Your desires are valid, no matter where you are on the spectrum.

However, it's important to recognize that many people seek external approval to validate their own self-worth. They rely on others' acknowledgment as confirmation that they're deserving and valuable. This is a fragile foundation on which to build your life, as we have discussed, because the moment someone withholds their acknowledgment, your intrinsic sense of worth falls through the floor. Now, that doesn't mean it's wrong to want a large community that appreciates you and your work, or parents who understand your unique blueprint and how you operate. It's absolutely OK to have those desires. However, they're not, and should never be used as, a yardstick that measures your worthiness. For example: *I can't be worthy if I've only received five likes on Instagram for the picture I posted.* Or, *My mum doesn't know what it means to see me and love me like I desire to be seen and loved, so there must be something wrong with me.*

The number-one person in line for seeing you in your Infinite Greatness is, and must be, you.

When we look at the fundamentals of wealth expansion, and the process we use to get the results we desire, we always start with the question – who? Who do I get to be in order to achieve the result I desire? If your result is 'seeing my own unique and Infinite Greatness,' we ask 'who do I get to be in order to see my greatness?'

While many of the people I work with desire to be seen as great, it's fair to say that acknowledging their own greatness doesn't feel comfortable at all. And on closer inspection, as soon as you look at who they are being on a day-to-day basis, it is clear that they are not looking at or living their life like their presence is a gift to the world. Perhaps you, too, don't see yourself as a walking, talking miracle. You don't celebrate your uniqueness as you frequently search for what you think might be wrong with you.

Why is this the case? At the core of it, and most frequently, it's that pesky fear thing again. Fear of people rejecting and then ultimately abandoning you if you get 'too big for your boots.' Fear that the voice in your head is right and you'll never be quite good enough, or as good as the rest – that feeling runs deep!

Sometimes that feeling is really subtle and other times it's wildly obvious where we don't feel we're standing fully in our power. So, if there's any part of you, even the smallest part of you, that doubts you're allowed to really see and know yourself in your greatness (spoiler: I haven't met a person yet that doesn't have some doubts), this chapter is going to show you how to shift this, while not getting lost in your ego or a need to prove to anyone else that you are great.

*Now is the time. Step up
and do things differently.*

Blocking yourself

Author and coach Tony Robbins, often cited as the godfather of personal development, says that to feel significant is one of our basic human needs – in his definition, what that means is to feel unique, important, special, or needed. When I think about my work and life, I desire for everyone I come into contact with to feel that. But significance at the deepest level isn't something that can be given to anyone; as with being seen, it's something that you as an individual first have to claim yourself. And the power in doing so is that when you choose it, it can't be taken away. When a person waits to be given significance by the people around them, the frequency they're actually hanging out in is lack, a sense of not enoughness, which stops us from consciously receiving what we actually desire.

A prime example of this happened on my 44th birthday. I definitely spent a portion of that day blocking myself from consciously receiving the love that I know is there and available for me at all times. Let me explain. On that day, despite the fact that my birthday is on the calendar and I'd spoken to the kids only the day before about it, when I woke up and got the kids up, there was nada for Mama. There were no cards, no gifts, there was nothing.

Now, to be fair to my children, the way it normally works on birthdays for me and for my ex-husband is that we'll rally them together and go and buy gifts for the other parent's birthday in advance. Sometimes we'll get a cake and do the cards and then, on the day, it's like, 'surprise' and the kids get excited to give their gifts.

That year, the kids were a bit older. My eldest, already in high school, received pocket money every week and would choose to buy gifts for friends on their birthdays with his own savings pot. So, there was a little more unvoiced expectation of him to take the lead, at least for himself.

And there was definitely an expectation of my ex-husband. So, when I woke up to nothing, I was disappointed. Which is a normal feeling to have, but what I allowed the lack of presents and thoughts to mean was that *nobody loves me; nobody cares about me; everyone takes me for granted; I'm going to die alone with six cats slowly feeding off my carcass.* (I'm a dog person by the way!) Even though I painted a relatively, 'I'm fine' face on it, I made the lack of acknowledgment of – come on, let's face it – what should be viewed as the greatest day in my children's lives, mean that nobody valued me. And so, when the kids eventually clocked on, and started singing 'Happy Birthday' to me, the meaning I'd attached to my feelings of disappointment meant I wasn't able to receive what they were able to give me at all.

Even though my highest desire was to be acknowledged and appreciated, because it wasn't packaged in the way that I wanted in the time frame that I desired, it wasn't enough. So, I blocked myself from receiving anything.

Of course, it didn't need to be that way. When it comes to receiving infinitely, what's true is that the more we take radical responsibility in what it is we desire to create and receive, the more we empower ourselves to create and receive. The truth is I don't need anyone to tell me of the significance or greatness of my role as the mother to my children. I see it and I live it every day. And on the days where I desire to be acknowledged, if it's truly important to me to be seen and treated in a certain way, rather than leaving it to chance with a bunch of kids and an ex-husband, I get to clearly tell people what it is that I desire.

Later, with my children, I did choose to explain that the two days where I'd deeply love for them to put some thought into me are my birthday and Mother's Day, and I know that I still get to lead on those things because I get to choose significance and greatness. And the more I choose to know my significance and greatness the more that knowing is reflected all around me. Everything always starts with you.

And do you know what? I had so much love gifted to me on my birthday by so many people in my life, my kitchen became a literal flower shop, but I was unable to receive any of it until I chose to recognize, appreciate, and choose significance and greatness for myself. Feel free to learn from all of my mistakes.

Environmental conditioning

Intellectually, this is a concept that most people can get behind: 'I have to see myself as great before other people can see me as great.' Oops! That's not actually the thing that I want you to get behind. There will have been at least one time in your life where you had the experience of someone telling you that you were amazing, or pretty, or you did really well at something but, on the inside, you're wanting the ground to open and swallow you up. It doesn't matter how many times you're told, you just don't believe it, so you can't receive it.

This Pillar isn't about you needing to see yourself as great so that other people will see you as great. This work is about you being willing to see yourself in your Infinite Greatness, so that when the people in your life and in your work reflect that back to you, you *can* receive it, because you already know it for yourself – #insideout.

The power in this, as with everything I'm sharing, is that it means your well-being is generated by you. If people want to compliment you and acknowledge you – great, and when you do this work, they absolutely will do. However, the acknowledgment is a bonus – you no longer *need* that cherry because you're already the most delicious cake and, most importantly, you know it.

Intellectually, I know you can get behind this too, but what's also true is, when we get serious about acknowledging that we're special, that we're walking miracles, all types of shizzle comes up.

Why? Because, in the beginning, acknowledging yourself can feel a lot like showing off and most of us learned that it's not OK to be a show-off. That we might not be loved if we shine too brightly. We remember the 'cool girl' in class who loved herself and made us feel inadequate, or the pretty girl that stood out and got bullied. There are so many times during our lifetime that we've felt judged for wanting to be seen or, dare I say it, been the person doing the judging. From experience, we've learned that it was better to play a smaller game. A game where we laugh at the same jokes as our friends, even when we don't think they're funny. We engage in conversations with people that make us want to slowly pluck out our eyelashes, one by one, because it feels safer than going out on a limb and saying, 'Actually I disagree with you about that. I think about things this way.' We think: *What if I'm not as great as I think I am and people make fun of me, or – even worse – I fall flat on my face?*

In the UK, we use the phrase 'tall-poppy syndrome.' It refers to the poppy that blooms taller than the uniform height of the other poppies in the field, and then needs to be chopped down so as not to create a visual disturbance in the uniformity of the poppy farm.

We see this happening frequently in the celebrity world via the media, where you have one person who's doing well in their career; they're seen and celebrated everywhere you look. And then one day something happens, the tide changes, and the once flavor-of-the-month is now anything but, and it seems as though everyone is out to get that person.

So, when we've seen this happen in our own lives and in the media that we consume, why would we really want to buy into the idea of 'celebrating your greatness' when the whole situation could end up misfiring in the worst possible way? Sure, there are still some people who pretend that they feel great and life is great (hello, Instagram highlight reel!), but on the inside feel like nothing and nobody. The problem presents itself differently, but is ultimately the same thing: They don't know their unique and Infinite Greatness.

Here's where the recommitment comes in if you truly desire to receive more.

Are you willing to see and do things differently?

We learned from childhood that it isn't safe to take up too much space or stand out from the pack. You're all too familiar from previous chapters with the concept that when you look at a baby, they don't need to do, be, or say anything to be perfection. As adults, we recognize the perfection in that baby to the core of their being, just because.

Depending on the context of our upbringing, if we're lucky, certainly for the first year of our lives, we're the center of our parents' or caregivers' universe. Now, if you come from a background where you didn't have that, what I'm moving on to say is still relevant; it's just that you learned to assimilate or try to fit in earlier than those who were graced with a more secure early start.

For those with a secure start, during our first year, perhaps even two, our perception is that we're the center of the universe, and everybody is there for our benefit alone. We expect every whim to be catered for. When we cry, it's up to our caregivers to provide for us – that is the expectation. We might be babies, but we hold the power.

By the time we reach the age of two, it's a different story. This is the point at which many parents decide that they need to get serious about teaching their child that it's just not possible to function in this world acting as though you are the center of it. This, for us as children, is a challenging concept to get our heads around, but as our parents persist for our greatest good, we learn. Now, of course, these are important lessons. I'm not suggesting we all grow up as a bunch of unruly narcissists who don't understand that sometimes a no is a no. However, the way our young brains are trained and interpret who we need to be and what we need to do to become socially acceptable – polite children who fall into line – doesn't set us up for knowing our greatness. There are too many caveats that slowly chip away at what makes us unique and most special.

We move from everything being incredible and within our power to, 'Hang on a minute, what do you mean? I said I want this, and you said, "no". What's going on?' Boundaries are now being put in place to keep us physically safe and to allow for the first stages of emotional maturity, which is needed. At the same time, we're learning that if we don't act or speak in a certain way, we might get scolded or isolated (when told to go away and think about what we've done). We start learning that in order to receive attention now, unlike when we were babies, we need to *do* stuff; to perform.

Again, depending on our caregivers, the required behavior might be right and appropriate – showing kindness, saying please and thank you, and so on. But what if we're naturally loud and inquisitive and our caregivers would rather we were quieter, or asked fewer questions? Then doing the 'right stuff' in order to receive the round of applause or proud look in their eyes might look different. We might suppress our natural nature to earn and keep our caregivers' approval. We learn that often love will feel conditional and, in order to feel loved or seen, we need to do things that align with out caregivers' desires rather than our own.

And if you've been brought up in a household where your caregivers were absent frequently, or consciously or unconsciously withdrew their love, your young brain is likely to have interpreted that as, 'What's wrong with me? What can I do better? What will make them happy?' And so, the cycle begins – failing to see yourself through anything other than the lens of your caregivers and their response to you.

Hello, conditional love

Combine this with Westernized religious conditioning, which tells us we're born imperfect, and depending on your own personal circumstances, a lack of equity, gender inequality, racism, sexism, ableism – the list could go on and on – it's not strange at all that most people aren't walking around the planet feeling like they're The Special One.

All of these micro- and macro-experiences of 'not enoughness' are remembered consciously and unconsciously in the mind and body. So, it's not surprising that the truth that we know when we're born – that we are all connected and that we're all greatness personified – starts to get eroded within the first two years of our lives. And then, when we go to school, the lesson is reinforced. When we do well in a test, we get more love from the teacher, more appreciation; or we receive adulation and acceptance from friends for acting in a certain way. We seek out that feeling of acceptance because we desire to feel included, acknowledged, and ultimately safe and loved.

As we get older and become adults, we're still acting out that story. What is it that I need to do in order to be loved? What is it that I need to do in order to feel seen, to be included, to be acknowledged? How can I put myself in the love-shaped box?

When I'm in the love-shaped box, then people will pour love into me and I'm going to feel good, I'm going to feel great, but the moment that person looks away, I no longer feel good and I no longer feel great. So, what do I need to do in order to get that attention again?

Most people go through their entire life trying to find this love-shaped box and they will tie themselves into pretzels to be the right thing in order to receive the love, in order to feel good about themselves.

We've forgotten the fundamental truth that we don't need to do anything or be anything to be great.

Catching yourself in the lie

That's why, when you say to me that you know you're great, as many of my clients do, I know that you want it to be true and I definitely want it to be true. But when you get really honest with yourself and look at your life, you'll be able to spot so many places where you choose the option of diminishing yourself and not showing up in your fullness, where you diminish your truth, quieten your voice, accept less than you truly desire, and take up less space in order to get the approval, the love, the acknowledgment, sometimes from the people that you love and other times from strangers from the internet who will never know the real you.

And I say all of this from a place of someone who's very much still in the work daily. I can start my day with a meditation feeling great, like I'm about to conquer the world, and yet by the time it's taken me to walk to the shower – approximately 20 steps – I find myself worrying or doubting myself about something; sometimes it's something completely insignificant, sometimes it feels like a genuinely big thing. But the truth is that if I really knew my greatness, I wouldn't doubt myself or worry about what the next person might think of me. I'd be able to consider the options in front of me not from a place of fear, but from a place of certainty that regardless of the end result, I'm still going to be – and always will be – worthy and deserving of love.

Now, while I'm certainly better at remembering this than when I was in my twenties, I'm by no means a guru when it comes to this next level of life mastery, and yet I have still created a level of abundance in my life that I never thought would be possible for a woman like me. Never. So, as I frequently remind myself, as I tell my kids, we're looking for progress over perfection. My progress shows up as being clear about where I am on the path, noting how I'm feeling, and catching myself when I take actions that are misaligned with how I desire to feel. My incredible mentors also pull me up when my actions aren't in alignment. And, as I'm on the same journey, it's easy for me to spot clients that are telling me, 'I'm doing the work,' when they're not. It's easy for me to look at their lives and see where there are so many more opportunities for them to lean even more deeply into knowing and living into their greatness.

As I've said, you don't need to get this perfect for it to make a huge difference, because you are intrinsically perfect. The number of times I have to choose to remember this, even in the writing of this book – the writing of this chapter – is a constant reminder that we are in this work together! So, with deep self-compassion, I want you to notice the difference between the times when you are thinking about knowing that you're truly great, when you're wishing you knew you were great, vesus *actually knowing* you're truly great. When you reclaim this 'knowing,' you're choosing to live from a whole different level of awareness.

What does this look like in practice? Owning your gifts. Appreciating that there isn't another human being on the planet that can say what you can with your un-replicable energetic signature. Flying your freakiness and loving it instead of diminishing it. Celebrating what makes you unique. Dropping comparison. Choosing to be inspired by another person's light instead of intimidated.

Of course, you'll have wobbles, but you'll be committed to catching yourself when you're having a moment, so that you can come back to truth. How do I know when I'm wobbling? I feel stressed. I'm anticipating what other people might be thinking. I'm trying to think how I can avoid being embarrassed. I'm worried about people thinking I might not be good enough, or being seen as a failure. My body feels tight and contracted. So, how do I disrupt the pattern? By noticing my dis-ease. Sometimes it will be in my mind; other times it will be in my body. To get back to my natural state of ease, I know that the first thing I have to do is pause and then bring my awareness back to how I'm breathing. Yes, your breath again – it's the most powerful tool and it's completely free! If I don't have the space to use the E in Motion Tool (p.80), then I simply bring my attention to the breath, deepening and slowing down my breathing.

Infinite invitation

One of the techniques that is useful in this circumstance is called the 4-7-8 breath. You simply breathe in to the count of four, hold the breath for seven, and exhale to the count of eight. It helps the nervous system to calm down and releases tension as it creates a sense of spaciousness in the body, as your cells respond to the increased oxygen in the blood.

In the space you create with the breath, you can ask yourself the following questions, to break the chain of thought and help you see things differently.

I use the acronym, IWWWI:

- **Is** this actually true?
- **What** would I like to be true?

- **W**hat would I choose for myself if I wasn't afraid?

- **W**hat would be the next most aligned step for getting one step closer to this reality?

- **I**s this the most expanded version of myself speaking?

This super-potent sequence of questions builds on each other and helps you to quickly shift your perspective. When it comes to asking yourself is this actually true, nine times out of ten, when you're really honest with yourself, you are catastrophizing. The thing you are freaking out about isn't very likely to happen, but let's say that by some freak occurrence your worst-case scenario did come true; how would you deal with it? You'd work it out and, depending on the type of person you are, it may or may not be useful to look at a top-level action plan. So, you can reassure your subconscious mind that you are in fact safe and good.

The drawback with a top-level plan is that you are putting all of your time and energy into a future memory that you don't want to recreate, but once you have a plan, you can justifiably tell your brain that it's OK to store it in a little compartment in your mind and that you only need to extract if the time calls for it. And that is the invitation I'm offering to every single one of you.

As we've established, Infinite Receiving and knowing your greatness is not about needing to be perfect at all, but more about how quickly you can catch yourself when you're in a pattern that isn't serving you, a pattern that is leaning into the old story that says that you need some kind of external validation for you to know that you're enough, and then shifting from that place. Most times when you ask yourself the question, 'Is this actually true?' the answer will be no.

The next question, 'What would I like to be true?', gets you back into the vision that you have for yourself and your dream. This question is a reminder that your intentions matter when it comes to consciously creating the world and the dreams you desire. Sometimes you'll find the mind will want to tell you that this thought is unfair, unrealistic, and all the things, and again you'll immediately start to doubt yourself.

This is when the next question comes in – the courage question: 'What would I choose for myself if I wasn't afraid?' Would you ask for what you want? Would you pick up the phone and ask for the sale? Make the pitch? If you can choose to go for it, irrespective of whether you're going to fall or fly, you put yourself in a much more favorable position than going round and round in circles just thinking about it. And here's the most beautiful thing: when you truly embody the Infinite Receiving philosophy, whether you're falling or you're flying, you're still in receiving mode. In the fall, there will always be incredible gifts and lessons for you that, if you take them on board and implement the learnings, will be invaluable to you.

The fourth question, 'What is the next most aligned step?', is an interesting one. Often, the thing that holds us back from making a move is the idea that we need to know all the steps and have a fully formed plan. I want to tell you that, while it might go against the conventional wisdom of mapping out your next five years in advance, it's usually just the next step that you need to take action on – particularly when you have been feeling stuck. And the next step is usually the thing that you have been doing your best to avoid.

As an entrepreneur, you can't avoid making mistakes – failure is part of the game. Strategizing to within an inch of your life to try to avoid failure or being seen to fail only slows you down. It won't stop the pain. So, why not just go for it, learn your lessons, apply the lessons, and go again? Because if your successes and failures don't determine your worthiness, what have you got to lose that you can't make up at some point down the line?

And then a final check in – question five: 'Is this the most expanded version of myself speaking?' Or, put another way: Are your new intentions coming from the part of you that knows who you are – the part of you that recognizes your limitless and Infinite Greatness – or are you still playing on the small side? If you are still playing small, go back to question three and ask yourself, 'What would I choose for myself if I wasn't afraid?' And do that.

Science-y stuff: Living out of the past and not the present

When you're not asking yourself questions like those above, it makes it that much more challenging for you to hold the space of greatness. So many people are building their future based on how they think and feel about what happened yesterday, rather than what's actually going on in the present moment. We base our actions on our memories, and memories are formed in very precise ways. In fact, if I were to write this process out as a formula this is what it would look like:

Experience + Emotion = Memories

This is why, even though we want to think and behave differently, it can feel so immensely challenging sometimes, because we're not operating from the place of possibility and what can happen. Frequently we're operating from past experiences without any conscious awareness at all because this is what we're literally wired to do.

It works like this: we have an experience, and it produces an emotion. The more heightened the emotion, the deeper the imprint of the experience that happens within our cellular memory. Put another way, the more potent the emotion, the more potent the memory will be. Some people believe that the body and the brain memory are completely integrated, others believe that the body has its own way of storing events separate from the brain. Either way memories are stored in both the body and mind both consciously and unconsciously.

The other thing that creates memories is repetition. The more frequently we repeat something or every time we're in learning mode, the brain creates new neural pathways. These pathways help us to remember and automate our responses to things. You have approximately 100 billion neural pathways in your brain that make up approximately 100 trillion neural connections. That in and of itself is just incredible. Doesn't that make you think, *Wow?!* It blows me away. Just because it's normal for humans, it doesn't make it less magnificent. Now, the more we repeat a habit the more dominant the pathway becomes until we can do tasks without even thinking about them. However, if we don't practice or use the skills we're acquiring, then the pathways ultimately disconnect. I used to watch an incredible yoga teacher called Barbara Curry when I first started my yoga journey, and she would say, 'If you don't use it, you lose it,' and this is what she was talking about. The more that we do something, the more it reinforces that memory.

The brain is designed to be as efficient as possible. Everything that you do goes into your memory bank. Then, whenever you do something even slightly familiar, the brain finds the corresponding neural pathway and makes it easier for you to recall something similar that has happened before, so you can anticipate or make an educated guess about what's going to happen next. It asks, 'When have we done this before?' and it pulls out that memory.

Which means that very rarely are you looking at what's in front of your face and thinking about the infinite number of possibilities for an outcome there could be for the scenario you're in. The brain quite literally doesn't function in that way. It looks back to see what you've seen or done before.

It's said that 46.9 percent of every single day, so almost half, we're operating from memory, on autopilot – we're not thinking at all. And, if we want to use really crude math, we spend one-third of the day sleeping, so less than a quarter of our time is actually spent consciously thinking; everything else is running on autopilot. So again, when you're wondering why it requires a whole other level of intention to remember that you are one of a kind, there will only ever be one of you, and that your unique fingerprint can never be replicated, this is the reason: you haven't been trained or trained yourself into thinking like this multiple days a week, for hours every day.

So, coming back to recognizing and acknowledging the magnificence of all of this magic before you have even opened your mouth to express anything gets to be more and more important to you every single day. You are a walking miracle.

Environment reinforcing biology

I share all of this because, as I have already said, since you were a small child – a two-year-old – you have been learning that you're not quite good enough unless you act in a certain way. And so much of your behavior since then has embodied that feeling of 'I'm not good enough.'

Then, your business demands that you come out into the world and say, 'I'm all that,' and you can't work out why it feels so freaking hard. Everything you have just read is why.

So, unless you are waking up every day with a clear intention to create something new in your life, you are operating from this past perspective, namely, *unless I do things in a certain way, unless I get a certain result, then I'm not good enough, I'm not lovable, I'm not great enough.* Or, *I can't possibly do that, because the last time I tried that I fell flat on my face. I'm just not ready to take the risk again.* But you need to remember that it feels unsafe to do something from the perspective of who you were, rather than who you have become and are becoming every day.

In truth, most people aren't waking up with this intention for growth. Most people are doing everything that they've always done daily up until this point. There are rare moments where you'll think, *I'm going to meditate,* or *I'm going to do some yoga,* and immediately you go back to the same old patterns, which create the same physical and emotional thoughts, feelings, and responses. It's a vicious cycle.

But not anymore. You get to start the process (it's not all going to shift overnight) of moving from the familiar, *I'm just not good enough*, to knowing at the core of your being that you are magnificent.

You are a unique and divine
expression of original Source.

Making the shift (new beliefs)

I feel passionately about this because I understand how much can shift, will shift, has the capacity to shift if you are able to genuinely tap into the knowing that you truly are incredible – 'I'm freaking amazing' – and not just from a cerebral place but from the inside out.

You get to start with baby steps, which looks like noticing. Noticing how many times you can catch yourself being falsely self-deprecating, saying things about yourself you'd be mortified to say about your best friend, and asking yourself the same questions you did at the beginning of this chapter. The Infinite Receiver ultimately chooses to love themselves deeply and that starts with how they speak to and about themselves. The more you can choose self-appreciation and wonderment even at the fact you have woken up each day, you'll slowly but surely increase your level of receiving.

When we look at ourselves on a moment-by-moment basis to catch ourselves slipping into the old patterns, we can ask ourselves, 'What do I know to be true?' When you can release the old stories and start the process of rewiring and reclaiming the truth of who you are and the truth of what is, this in turn is going to increase your capacity to receive.

Transformational Tools

What shifts for you right now when I ask you: 'Does it astound you that you are made from the same compounds as the stars? How do you feel? How does that feel in your body?' Jot down your answers in your journal.

Did you know the odds of you having been born are one in 400 trillion? How does it make you feel when you hear that number? You're one in 400 trillion and there's nobody on this Earth, even if you're a twin, who's the same individuated expression as you.

So, when you look at how you have been today, have you appreciated that you are one in 400 trillion? Have you acted as though you are made of stardust? Have you taken a moment to acknowledge that you are made from the same particles as every single part of this planet? Have you acted as though you are part of this universal tapestry of life? If your answer is 'no,' what do you imagine might have been or felt different about your day if you *had* remembered to tap into the energy that is carried within this wisdom?

For those of you who can truthfully answer 'yes,' what has been different about the way that you've felt and in the way that you have shown up today in comparison to the days where you've been in the 'just got to get shizzle done' mode? Write it down in your journal.

For the rest of you, when you think about sharing from that place of 'I'm one in 400 trillion,' how does it feel to share from that space? Write it down in your journal.

When people say that personal development is hard work, I say that it's way harder to go through life not realizing that you are a walking miracle. Trust me: The hard work is choosing *not* to live your life and show up in your business from that place of *I am one in 400 trillion and I'm starting to recognize that I'm pretty freaking special.* When I think of the person who chooses that, I think, *Wow, what a waste.*

For me, there's no better example of what it means to be an Infinite Receiver than when I share the examples of where I trip up, or where I get stuck, on this because in my sharing, you're receiving.

Even as I was writing this chapter on Greatness Amplification, which means so much to me, I was like, 'OK, what can I do to make this even better? What can I do to really make it land? What can I do, because I want to make it perfect so that you will see me as perfect?' You see – right there, I've forgotten that everything unfolds perfectly for the highest good of everyone at all times. Wanting the message to be communicated as well as it can be is good; needing it to land in a certain way so that you will think that I am a better person is a whole other story. In real time, you can see how easy it is to forget. How easy it is to think: *If I just made this a bit different, then it will be good enough, and that will mean that I am good enough.* The work is to remember, regardless of how the words land, that I am complete, I am whole, and I am enough anyway. It's the work of a lifetime and I'm here for it.

So, even if you feel that you know your greatness, that you've got this now, I want you to hear me when I say that I catch myself in the old loop frequently, even though I've created a level of love, abundance, joy, and wealth in my life that I never believed was possible. If you're anything like me, then there's always the opportunity to go deeper into knowing your enoughness.

I am full, I am whole, I am complete
and enough now.

Transformational Tools

I have one last exercise for you in this chapter, so please answer the following questions in your journal:

- Is there anything worth sacrificing being full of yourself for?

- Is there anyone on this planet that is worth sacrificing being full of yourself for?

I'm fully expecting the parents among you to write, 'well, maybe my child.' If so, ask yourself the question, 'Is there anything in this world you'd want your child to sacrifice being full of themselves for?'

OK, let that marinade for a while. Remember, this is a journey. That's why I pointed out at the start that you're not going to get it overnight, but the commitment starts here. The commitment to catch yourself when you're diminishing, the commitment to catch yourself when you're wobbling, the commitment to catch yourself when you're feeling like screaming.

We start amplifying our codes of greatness by recognizing the miracle of who we are. That's where it starts.

The second step to amplifying your greatness and so increasing your capacity to receive is outlined in the next chapter.

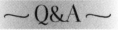

Q: *If I were completely in my greatness, I'd easily be able to lean back and trust. How do you master leaning back?*

A: I can easily tell, through how my body feels, when I'm pushing and when I'm forcing something. And it doesn't feel good. I know that if I'm going to do my best work, it's going to feel good in my body. And if it doesn't feel good in my body, then the question I ask myself is, 'How would I approach this if I was going to allow it to be easy?' And then I listen to that answer. And then I do that answer.

Faith + Action = Miracles

Chapter 7

Pillar of Infinite Greatness – Recognizing the Miracle in Others

In the previous chapter, we started the process of amplifying our Infinite Greatness codes and recognizing the miracle of who we are. In this second part of the Pillar of Infinite Greatness, we dive deep into recognizing the miracle of who everybody else is.

One of the things that holds people back from really shining their light is that there's often a belief that your light might detract from others. But the truth is: even though you are special, so is everyone you'll ever come into contact with. The idea that if you shine too brightly, others' lights will appear dimmer is another learned idea that comes from flawed thinking. It comes from the thinking of comparison. It comes from the thinking that the real game we're playing is a zero-sum game, where ultimately there's only one winner.

This thinking is scarcity-minded and it certainly doesn't embody the message of Infinite Receiving. Instead, look to the yogic tradition, where every class ends with the phrase 'Namaste,' which means 'the light in me sees the light in you.' This is the truth. Every single human on this planet carries greatness and when you are willing to see yourself as great, irrespective of what you have or have not achieved, you can see it in others, too.

It's way more challenging to see someone in their Infinite Greatness when you can't touch it in yourself. It's not impossible, but it is more challenging because when we don't know our own greatness, we focus on results. We look for what a person is doing or achieving first, then compare it to ourselves, and then others. In the process, we often completely ignore the fact that we are looking at another walking, talking miracle who has something to teach or remind us just from merely existing.

This means that, depending on what we perceive another person to have achieved, we either diminish them or we end up putting them on a pedestal. Sometimes this makes us feel inadequate and want to shy away; other times we hope to be seen as cooler, happier, funnier, richer than we perceive ourselves as being. Either way, we are missing the point that someone else's greatness is something we could never add to or diminish with our words or behavior, and we are no longer in the frequency of Infinite Greatness. And in the case of the latter example, we're in 'prove it' energy. But the truth is that there's nothing to prove to anyone, not even ourselves. We all come from the same Original Source and every individual's intrinsic value is priceless. If someone has a bigger bank balance or more accolades, all that means is that they have a bigger bank balance and more accolades. It doesn't make them more worthy and deserving than you as a human. And recognizing and applying this in your life, and to everyone you meet, has the capacity to change everything.

It means that you treat the person who's collecting your trash with the same reverence for the miracle of their humanness as you would the Dalai Lama. It means that you see the person who invests their last £97 in your product as just as valuable as the person who's going to invest £20k or more on your services, because you recognize the greatness in both.

One of my fundamental beliefs that has served me greatly is the idea that there's no separation between ourselves and anything on the planet. There's an energetic thread that runs through us all that means my actions impact the whole and the whole's actions impact me. This is as true for us humans as it is for the sun, the moon, and the stars. There is no separation. We all originate from the same Source. Science reinforces this when we see that our DNA, which contains carbon, nitrogen, oxygen, and phosphorus, were all formed in the stars. Another miracle.

And yet even though we're all connected, nothing and no one is replicated. There's not one single replication. We're all unique, individuated expressions of God, The Universe, Source, whatever feels most aligned to you, and that again is another mind-bender. It's absolutely incredible. We're all coming from the same place, but we're all slightly different, by which I mean completely unique.

What's interesting is, in the quest for being seen as great, very few people take into consideration all the magic I've just shared. Instead of celebrating their uniqueness, people try to emulate the people they think are great and successful, completely ignoring the magnificence of their own unique blueprint. Where once it was the outside forces that chipped away at your remembering, every time you try to be a bit more like someone else, instead of being a bit more like you, you miss the entire point. This is why I want you to be more and more full of yourself. It's the only thing that makes sense.

And from this place of fullness, you get to observe everyone else's fullness. From this place of being able to see the miracle in everybody else, you also get to finally start choosing and acknowledging the miracle in you. From this perspective, either everybody's a miracle or nobody is. Which world do you want to live in? I know which one I'm choosing.

But what about people who do bad things?

This is where again you get to choose whether you are willing to recommit to Infinite Receiving, because when we choose this life, you can of course dip your toe in and only work with the things that make you feel comfortable, but then you barely scratch the surface of what's possible for you. So, when it comes to people who do bad things, what can we learn?

It's important to say that on the spectrum of bad things, the measure is far and wide, but in my experience of dealing with the bad things that have happened to me personally, what has been most liberating for me is going back to the beginning of a person's life and being willing to see them in their humanity. Contrary to many Western-based religions, I don't believe that every human was born a 'sinner.' I don't believe that people were born bad.

Everyone has the capacity to do bad things, because we're part of all things. We're part of the Whole. If there is truly no separation, then there's no separation between the good and the bad. However, the context – the environment a person was brought up in, what they were trained to believe about themselves, all the opportunities a person had to learn the things that could elevate the way that they see themselves and the world, or didn't have to unlearn the things that didn't serve them – contributed to them not knowing their intrinsic value and not seeing it in other people. In certain contexts, everyone is capable of doing bad things.

How should we respond to people who do bad things, then? With compassion and by releasing judgment. It's easy to say, but difficult to do, so go back to the truth that every baby was born worthy and deserving. By choosing not to dehumanize people, we have the capacity to change so much conflict, hate, and anger. To recognize someone's humanity, even when their actions might be completely abhorrent to you is to be willing to separate the human from the action. And, while you may never condone or like the behavior of a person, if you're willing to think about that person's context and see them in their humanness, you will change your entire life.

Transformational Tools

Take a few minutes to reflect on and answer these questions:

- If I knew my light couldn't detract from anyone else's, what would I choose to do differently today?

- If I knew my light supported others in shining even more brightly, how would I choose to show up?

Then try saying out loud: 'I choose every day to be more full of myself. I choose significance.'

Write down what that means for you. How does it feel?

Fullness and greatness

For me, when I think about what it means to be full of life, I see the fizz you get when you pop a bottle of champagne. It's overflowing. It's all encompassing. There are no limitations.

It's not so much even about living life, it's BE-ING life, and being in full recognition that life is running through your veins and that is such a privilege. It's a deep appreciation and acknowledgment that there's not a person on the planet that has your unique perspective, your voice, your blueprint. The more you're willing to honor that, the more you get to experience the fullness of yourself, And the more full of yourself you become, the more your unique greatness shines through. As Abraham Hicks has said, who would you want to be full of, if not full of yourself?

If saying 'full of yourself' still doesn't feel fully aligned for you to say, then I invite you to say, 'full of greatness' or 'full of life' – go for it. I love to say, 'full of myself.' For me, it feels a little rebellious and equates to limitless expansiveness.

And at the same time, I can see why some people might still find this idea a little challenging. We've grown up in a world, where the winner takes all, there's only one spot on the top of the podium and, unless you're going for Olympic gold, the person who goes for it, who claims it (and even when you are going for Olympic gold) can sometimes be seen as being a bit of an egomaniac, and this isn't a good thing. The person at the top is quite tangibly better than everyone else. We're back to the zero-sum game again.

But what if, outside of a racetrack, the idea of the winner taking all isn't the game we're playing anymore? What if there's enough space on the podium for everyone to be full of themselves, in the same way that one person's light can't detract from the light of another? What if it's not, 'I'm full of myself and there's only space for you to be half of you, because I'm taking up all of the room'? Even though that is the story that many of us have grown up with? We're all walking this almost-impossible line of needing to prove that we're the best, while simultaneously needing to make sure we're not too much, so that no one else feels too uncomfortable or not enough in our presence. It's exhausting.

Imagine how different life would be if, when you heard about someone getting excited about a new thing that is happening in their life, your first response was, 'Wow that's amazing for you,' and your second thought wasn't one of negative comparison. What if you could celebrate their unique ability to nail whatever they have nailed and know that it doesn't diminish any part of who *you* are, or what you are doing – regardless of where you are on the journey right now? Or make where *you* are heading any less meaningful to you? Imagine how different life would be if you knew you had nothing to prove, not even to yourself. Just imagine. Being able to receive more is choosing this knowing for yourself again and again and again and being willing to catch yourself compassionately when you wobble or forget.

I am magic. I know I am magic. And
no one can stop my magical ass.

Are you in, or are you out?

Here's the thing: I want you to know that the invitation to be fully expressed is not a light invitation. The commitment required for you to fully express yourself is huge. It's a daily intention and a practice that I'm still in the process of allowing and figuring out for myself. The reason I say, 'I choose to be full of myself; it's safe for me to be full of myself. And, even if it's not safe, I still choose that for myself,' is because not every space is like the forum on my website. Not everybody is on this path. Or they may be on this path, but they may be further back on their journey. They may not be ready to step in. They may not understand. You may be misunderstood. You run the risk of people saying, 'Well look at you. Who do you think you are?'

And the question is, are you willing to see yourself and your greatness, anyway?

It's a biggie.

This is about choosing the life that *you* desire to live – for you. Somebody said to me the other day in a tutorial, 'I get frustrated because I don't feel like I'm even scratching the surface of my infinite potential.' And I get it because when your potential is infinite, where do you even start? It's big. Owning your greatness is definitely a good place to begin, though. It starts with you, every day, enquiring how much more full of yourself you can allow yourself to be. And, sure, some of those people around you who are living in the old story of who you were and who you should be, won't get it or like the new version of you, and they may push back against the change.

Or, they won't understand because, even though Infinite Receiving is available to everybody, the real magic happens when we add our consciousness and intention into the mix. It's about consciously co-creating an existence where you are the center of the give-and-receive cycle on a day-to-day basis. You get to decide if you are willing to be *that* person and not everybody is ready. For some, it feels safer to do what they have always done. But as these people observe you changing your life, little by little, shining just a little brighter, claiming what you desire a little more confidently, they notice. Often, they aren't even sure what they're noticing, but they see it and they feel it. And the more they feel it, the more they'll become curious, and so the ripple effect begins – because the more you shine, the more you give permission to others to shine too.

The more you say yes to accepting your greatness, the more you'll notice the type of magical things I mentioned in the introduction, like strangers in shops feeling compelled to ask you what you do, complimenting you on your hair, your radiance, random things. People will also comment on the results, your external appearance, but what they're really feeling is that you have chosen to be a portal for greatness. And, as you commit to leaning into that for the highest good of everyone you come into contact with, the ripple becomes a tidal wave. This is a big deal. It's not always going to feel easy, but the rewards for you saying, 'I'm on this path, let's go; let's live this life to the optimum in my unique greatness,' are undeniable.

It's also why having a community of like-minded people who get what you're doing is so important. On the hard days when it's easier to forget what you're doing and why you're doing it, you'll have a whole group of people who can reflect why this is important to you. They can remind you of who you have become because of this work and, more importantly, who you are becoming each and every day. This is why I love my own community in The Portal so deeply. These are the people who are in it and doing the work. These are the people saying, 'as we stand in our greatness, we inspire other people to stand in their greatness, because when they see it in us, they believe it is possible for them.' My feeling is that by reading this book, you are saying, 'I desire to be one of the leaders who supports other people in knowing themselves, being themselves, but we go first.'

Transformational Tools

To end this chapter, I want to leave you with some journaling. The question I'd like you to answer is below. I'm going to pose it in various ways - choose which sits best with you. Jot down your immediate takeaway, let it marinade, and then answer it again.

- Am I great? Am I great now?

- Am I willing to know myself from greatness now?

- Who would I be if I allowed myself to be in my greatness now?

- Do I believe it to be true that I'm made of stardust?

I appreciate you deeply. Namaste.

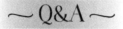

Q: *Can I be great in my imperfections?*

A: Of course! Perfection only exists in the dictionary. If we needed to be 'perfect' before we could recognize our greatness or receive infinitely, this book wouldn't exist. The invitation is to notice when you are not living your life in honor of your uniqueness and your greatness. And when you notice that you've forgotten that you are a walking, talking miracle, pause, offer yourself some deep compassion, and ask yourself what you would do if you were to give yourself permission to live from your greatness; what would you choose for yourself?

Faith + Action = Miracles

Chapter 8

Pillar of Infinite Support – Rooted in Receiving

The last two chapters were big ones – don't worry if it's taking a little while for the message of the Pillar of Infinite Greatness to land. My hope for you is that you'll come back to this book again and again and again, each time allowing these truths to penetrate deeper into your cells and become part of you. My intention with the last chapter was for you to start seeing yourself in your greatness and being aware of the magic of who you are on a daily basis. Owning your greatness isn't about what you are doing. It's about who you are being. It's about recognizing that you truly are a living, walking, talking miracle. When you start to see yourself fully, you'll notice that you speak differently, you write differently, you show up in the world differently. You feel inspired, because you're not trying to prove to yourself or anyone else that you're enough, and you get to experience yourself in more and more of your fullness.

In this chapter, we're exploring the Pillar of Infinite Support, which is all about allowing yourself to be supported both in the very tangible physical experience of your daily life, and by the less tangible invisible support team that runs through the Universe, which some people refer to as Life Force, the Divine, Source, or God (insert whichever term aligns with your beliefs). The goal is to create an environment that leaves you feeling infinitely supported in every moment of every single day.

To get this show on the road, let's start with a mini grounding exercise. You can listen to this guided meditation in the *Empower You Unlimited Audio* app (search 'Meditations for Infinite Receiving'). Or you can record it in your own voice and play it back.

Transformational Tools

If it feels good and safe for you to do so, just allow your eyes to gently close and focus on your breath for a moment or so. Gently breathing in and increasing your sense of calm and ease, releasing any worries and stresses or anxieties.

My invitation to you is to really be here now. Recognize that, in this moment in time, everything is good. You're breathing, you're alive, you've given yourself the gift of presence, and this is all perfect.

Allow anything that is not serving you in your highest and in your best just to fall away.

Bring your attention to your heart space. As you feel the heart expand, just notice how the oxygen moves around the inner workings of the heart, as well as the outside.

I invite you to open the heart just a little more and, as soon as you set the intention to open, notice the shifts that immediately take place. Whatever you notice, all is welcome. Just notice the smallest or even the largest of changes that take place. You may notice parts of your body expanding, your heart space expanding, or perhaps it's a contraction. All is perfect, all is welcome, without any judgment at all. Give yourself full permission to receive these words with an open heart and an open mind and allow yourself to draw exactly what you need to expand into your next level of receiving.

When you're ready, not a moment before, just allow your eyes to gently open, coming back fully present to the here and the now.

Let's get started

My key objective for this chapter is that you anchor yourself in the knowing that in every step you're taking, you're not alone. My intention is that, once you've read and integrated this chapter, you'll know that you can't mess 'it' or anything up. Even if you feel like you're in the biggest pile of poop right now, you are still not messing it up. Every single lesson that you are experiencing is needed for your expansion. That is what I want you to know. Everything is needed and useful for the next step in your journey.

This conversation about allowing yourself to feel and be fully supported goes hand in hand with being willing to release the desire to control all the things. So, here goes:

My name is Suzy Ashworth, and I am a recovering Control Freak.

Hands up if you're with me. As business owners, we often start out wearing all the hats. Even if you're not wearing all the hats right now, there was a time when you were the bookkeeper, the accountant, the CEO, the marketing director, the tea-maker, the personal assistant, customer-service assistant, and advertising department. When you team that with your roles as chief bottle-washer, parent, sibling, friend, cousin, and child at home, there are a lot of instances where you had to be the person that took control of making sure that things got done, or things wouldn't get done.

When it comes to increasing your capacity to receive in your business and in your life, though, you are going to have to let go of the reins and the desire to hold it all, do it all, and control it all. You can't receive infinitely if you're in control mode. You can't allow more in if you need to touch all the things in order to feel safe and secure. You can't receive everything that is available to you if you are trying to hold everything all the time.

The biggest revelation for most of my clients is how much they would actually love to be receiving more support in their lives, but they've had so many times where they have been let down that they stopped asking for and accepting help, even though they now have many capable people who would love to offer their support.

When it comes to allowing more in your business, especially when you're looking to grow your impact, the more you try to do it all by yourself, the more difficult it is.

I have a different relationship with support now than I did 10 years ago. It's been a journey and every time I'm looking to grow, this is a Pillar that I come back to again and again and again. I have a very beautiful relationship with support now because of the Infinite Receiving work I've done and because of this awareness. But it wasn't always like this.

In the past, I needed to do it all myself. I 'decided' at a very young age that it wasn't safe to rely on other people to do things for me or be there for me. I use the term 'decided' because, on reflection, I know that it was as a baby, before I could even speak, that I had my first experience of not being supported in the way I desired. It was when I was put into foster care at the age of three months old. Going from being in the arms and smell of my biological mother, the person who had carried me in her womb for nine months, into the arms of another woman, and immediately having all I had known since being in the womb just vanish, would no doubt have impacted my sense of safety and trust. From a processing perspective, this would have been a confusing and traumatic experience for baby Suzy, even though I had been fortunate enough to be placed in the hands and hearts of the most incredible foster carers.

Although I was not consciously aware of this until recent years, the wound created by the experience of having my original support system removed unexpectedly created a desire to protect my heart and myself from experiencing that type of disappointment and pain again. While everyone has a different story to tell about support, I've seen from my clients' stories that most people are able to track back to something early on in life that demonstrates that sometimes the people that you rely on the most can't be trusted. If you want to feel safe, you need to be the person that takes control. It's what makes you an excellent candidate for owning a business. But, as always, our greatest strengths can also be our biggest weaknesses if we don't bring conscious awareness to how we're using our superpowers.

What's interesting about the need to do it all yourself is that the frequency that intention vibrates at sits with both control and scarcity. It's the story that if you don't do it all, it will all fall apart. Other people aren't as capable as you, won't do it as well as you, you'll save more time if you do it yourself. If you only take one thing from this chapter, it's recognizing that while you are telling yourself the story that it must be you, you're vibrating on the frequency of lack. And that means you're a match for more lack in your life.

Can you see how different life could be if you chose to see people not just in their greatness, but actually let them support you, too? I know, wild concept isn't it? Take a breath if you need to.

There are two different types of support that I want to talk to you about. First, we have the extremely important ground-level support, and then in the next chapter we're going to talk about Universal support. Both have the capacity to change the way you do *all the things* and the way you feel moment by moment.

The less I do, the more I receive.

Ground-level support

The biggest thing that shifted for me in terms of ground-level support is that the more support I allow in, the less I do, and the more I receive.

I'm not sure exactly when I first set that intention (the less I do the more I receive), but it was strange because it was diametrically opposed to anything I had learned growing up, and not aligned to the experience of life that I had ever lived up until that point. What I had learned from my parents was a work ethic. They worked their butts off, they cleaned, did odd jobs, delivered papers; Mum was an Avon lady. I watched them work hard and earn just enough to keep food on the table and provide my sister and me with a two-week holiday in a chalet at a holiday camp each year. In my own career, what I saw was that when I put my foot down and picked up the phone more, asked for the sale more, did more things, pushed on through, I got better results. So, it feels important to acknowledge that I know pushing and bulldozing your way through works. I know because I've done it. But honestly, I was forced into deciding that the less I work, the more I receive was going to become true for me and become part of my identity, because of The Wealth Trifecta and Experiential Wealth.

What I wanted to create professionally, alongside being a mum of three children who I actually want to be an active and present mum for, meant that if I tried to do more and more things, something would have to give. And I wasn't willing to sacrifice myself or my family. There's no point in making all the money in the world if you're working so hard that you can't actually live and enjoy your life, right?

Transformational Tools

'The less I do the more I receive.' How does that sentence sit with you? Take some time to contemplate what comes up for you in your journal. If it activates you in a less-than-positive way, first look at what feels true for you right now and then write about what you'd like to be true for you when you think or say this phrase out loud. You do actually get to choose.

Reluctance to ask for help

As with many of the beliefs and the stories in our lives, they're rooted in something that has happened in childhood or something that has had a deep emotional impact on us at whatever period. I've noticed among my predominantly female client base that there's frequently, but not always, a reticence to ask for help and support. Usually, it's because they're running stories like: 'If I don't do it, it won't get done; I have to hold all the things; nobody else knows how to do it; it's quicker if I do it; I don't have the finances to hire someone else to do it for me; it's expected, and I just do it; I feel guilty asking someone else to do it; actually, I like doing all the things: it makes me feel useful and needed.' Let that last reason sink in. Are you also controlling situations or blocking other people from doing things for you to protect your feelings? It's a very useful protection mechanism – until it's not.

Protective control shows up in a variety of ways. It might be family members offering help around the home, but you say no, or take over midway through the task, because they're not doing it properly or it just feels easier to do it all yourself. In business, you refuse to hire, or you might hire but then refuse to delegate, because you don't want them to feel overwhelmed or to give them too much too soon. Or, you're just not quite sure what to give them, or you feel that the amount of time it would take to explain the task or to train someone to do it (which, of course, will be at a substandard level to the way you'd do it, right?) is just not worth the hassle.

In the home, this can frequently show up as victim energy or martyr energy. It sounds like, 'Nobody listens to me'; 'I have to do it all'; 'Nobody cares.' In business, it's working ridiculous hours doing things that are outside your 'zone of genius' – as Gay Hendricks, author of *The Big Leap,* talks about; things that it would be far more efficient and time-saving to delegate, which would have the impact of creating the much-needed time and space for the activities that are actually going to create infinitely more leverage in your business. Where do you see this pattern in your life and business?

The question of where I can allow myself to be even more deeply supported is a question that I'm always asking myself, because the bigger the impact I want to create, the more hands are needed to help bring my vision of the parent and the CEO I want to be to life.

And when you look at this from a purely financial perspective, it's just not feasible if every time you set an intention to double your income, you also have to double the number of hours you're working. There just aren't enough hours in the day. So, here's a hard truth that was reflected to me by one of my mentors, Regan Hillyer, many years ago. She said to me, 'Not everybody gets what they want, but everybody gets what they tolerate.' What I took from this was that if I desired to create a bigger impact, live my life to the full, and enjoy time with my family, then I'd need to be prepared to ask for support and willing to allow it in when that support showed up. This was a mic-drop moment for me.

If you have been willing to tolerate not being supported in your home or business, then that is on you. If you're anything like me then that revelation probably feels a little uncomfortable, I know. And there are reasons, good reasons, you have been willing to tolerate a lack of support up until now. One reason that I see time and time again is distraction. If you are so busy doing everything for everyone else, you're not going to have the time or the energy to do the things you actually want to do, are you? And that can be an incredible get-out clause.

Transformational Tools

Think of an area of your life where you know you need or would love to have more support, and then answer the following question in your journal:

How does it serve me to stay unsupported?

Look for reasons that it will actually protect you/keep you safe by staying busy or distracted in this area.

Taking it all on in business

What this looks like in business is refusing to hire. The story you tell yourself is that having a team of people feels hard, but if you try to be the marketing director, accountant, virtual assistant (VA), and umpteen other roles, then it makes it extremely difficult to grow. Even if at the beginning of your business it did make financial sense for you to take on the lion's share of the work, it eventually becomes massively inefficient, because you're doing so many things that are outside your scope of genius. You're doing things that other people could be doing better, saving you time and creating space for you to do the things that make you more money.

In my experience of personally hiring, firing, dealing with resignations, and forging real relationships with the team I've built and rebuilt over the last 10 years, as well as supporting my clients who are doing the same: Hiring support in your business is definitely one of the most challenging things you'll need to learn how to do. There's a steep learning curve and often many missteps along the way that, if you let them, will reinforce the old story that you are better off just doing it on your own. But if you're committed to consciously creating your life and living in Infinite Receiving mode, you need to stop attempting to do it all alone. If you're on your third VA or customer service person, don't make the decision that 'the right person' doesn't exist or think that there's something wrong with you. It's a process and it might just mean that you need some support in learning how to hire more support. And that doesn't have to cost you. Have you heard of something called YouTube? Of couse, you have! It's one of the greatest free resources both for business owners who are just starting up and those who are way past the bootstrapping phase. It's time to accept more support, even if that means just watching a video or two.

If you're ready to hire, start by creating a really beautiful intention about what it is that you're building. This is your vision. Alongside the vision you have for your business, take the time to reconnect with the intentions you have for life in general. Think about the impact you want to have in the world and let yourself feel excited and fired up by what it is that you're creating. Get clear on how you want to feel in your business on a day-to-day basis. Stressed, overworked, and underpaid is generally not the vibe. But excited, focused, and creative might be a good starting point for you.

This is you consciously curating, creating, and elevating your experiential wealth as you hone your future vision, and it shouldn't take long for you to realize that if this is going to become your reality, then you are going to require support. Because if you are running around doing all the things in your business, in a way that leaves you too depleted for your life, everyone in your personal life, including you, is going to feel it.

When you have clarity here for yourself, be willing to ask the people you are interviewing for a role – even when they are part-time and working with other people alongside you – the same question about their vision as you asked yourself: What do they want? Are they excited about your vision? If they seem almost as excited about your vision, and their future vision aligns with what you are creating, it's a powerful indicator that you might have a match that goes way beyond skill set.

It might take kissing a few frogs before you find the perfect person in this way, but when you do, you'll have sown the seeds for a beautiful relationship that goes way beyond the money that you're paying them. This puts you in a unique position because as they feel you see and honor their greatness, they see, feel, and honor you in yours. Immediately here, we experience a whole different quality of energy exchange. You're giving and you're receiving, and it gets to be beautiful, but to get to that place, you must decide that it's not just possible to have incredible people supporting you, it's possible for you.

It's safe for me to be infinitely supported.

Transformational Tools

In my experience, there's always a way to allow more support in our personal lives, too. I want you to ask yourself, when you think about your life right now, is there at least one person you can think of that actually wants to help you, that you won't allow to even though they want to?

Most of the time, when I ask this question, 99 percent of clients can immediately think of at least one person. Often, it's parents or partners; sometimes colleagues; occasionally, kids. On one occasion, a client said that there was nobody in her life who wanted to support her more. Ironically, that person had been part of the client group for the Infinite Receiving 6 week program, so I knew that wasn't true because the entire group, including me, wanted to support her. And, from things that she had said in the group, I suspected that her partner was keen to support her more, too. But she was blocking all of us because she wouldn't allow herself to see or ask for the support that was available.

There are so many people like this. I was like this! Now, the thing is, there might be valid reasons why you haven't asked that person for support in the past, but first ask yourself the question: are those reasons still valid today? Or are you still protecting yourself from an old disappointment?

You might say, actually those reasons are still valid and then you get to ask yourself: if there's one person that I know that would be willing to help me, there's got to be another. Who would that person be? Ask. And if you are in a situation where you feel truly isolated, firstly widen your perspective, while remembering it's not possible to be able to see the greatness in all other people and simultaneously believe that there's no one on the planet who wants to or is willing to support you.

Secondly, know that you are picking up and continuing to read this book for a specific reason; you have found these words at this time, so that they can support you in this next chapter of your life. Start noticing all the small things in your life that are helping you move forward and start to collect evidence daily of even the smallest of things that people do, consciously and subconsciously, that support you. The next time someone offers to get the door for you, help you with your bags, or wants to do anything for you that you'd appreciate, say yes. And notice how many more times you can say yes to receiving in this way instead of deflecting it.

So, on a practical level, whether you're being a burning martyr in the home or a superhero in the office, I want you to shift the story to knowing that in the life that you are living, you are, or get to be, infinitely supported in everything you do. And doesn't that feel like a delicious intention to get your energy behind?

I attract the perfect people at the perfect time, more and more in my life.

Forgiveness

Given that our belief around having to do it all for ourselves is often rooted in childhood and, especially, being let down by a parent or caregiver, it's small wonder that many of us are most resistant to accepting support from a parent.

Depending on the context of your upbringing, the support you get from your parents might not look like the 'storybook' version of family relationships. And that's okay. It is still totally possible to create some sort of structure where you are able to receive in some way from them. But before that is possible, we have to create space. There has to be forgiveness first.

What works for me is choosing to know that every step, every lesson up to and including today was, and is, required. I also think about the context that my parents were brought up in, and I choose to release judgment. While it's not the easiest philosophy to adopt at times, especially when the lessons we encounter are heartbreaking, on the other side of the pain is peace. Sometimes that peace is the medicine needed for both sides to allow for a new relationship to be built that includes support. And, other times, forgiveness is just forgiveness.

What I found to be true is that when I was willing to let myself be supported, I wasn't only forgiving my parents, but everyone who I had ever felt let down by in my life. And as I chose to forgive more, I noticed more of a sense of freedom, personal freedom, because I was no longer using my energy in defensive mode to protect myself.

This is the way that I look at things: The amount of energy that is released when we stop holding on to the old hurts and stories of the past supports us when it comes to creating a whole new way of living and interacting with the world.

Perhaps you've experienced relationships in your life that had a purpose, but that purpose has now come to an end. I don't have a relationship with my birth father. I hold no animosity toward him; and that's important to me because I did for a long time and my resentment toward him blocked me from receiving love and support from others. For those of you who feel that your parents desire to support you, yet you're somehow blocking them because of old stories that you are unwilling to let go of, then forgiveness work and truly believing that every lesson, every step, was required in order for you to be here can be transformative. Choosing to forgive and release the old creates so much freedom and allows you to receive so much more.

You are not an island

And, for those of you who simply feel like you don't need support, I get it. For many years, I unconsciously ran my life with a very hard exterior. I smiled, I danced, and I was good fun, but beneath the smile was a very hard exterior. Like, 'Don't f*** with me. I got this; I see you.'

The hard exterior that I had been using to protect my heart from further heartbreak meant that I found it almost impossible to allow myself to ask for support, and I also made it difficult for people to realize when I needed help, because my mask was, 'I'm so strong; I'm so capable; I don't need anything.' I was creating the self-fulfilling prophecy that I couldn't rely on anyone other than myself. The reality is that this mindset served me really well, until it didn't. Until I realized just how exhausted I'd become by keeping everyone at arm's length and feeling like I was doing it all alone – even when I was in a partnership. Always needing to hold on, to protect and defend my heart, just so I didn't get hurt again.

If I'm not being conscious, this old pattern of behavior can still sometimes creep through. But what has changed the game for me is softening. The type of softening that can only occur when you allow yourself to trust enough to be held; held by life and held by the people who love you.

If you're one of those people who finds themselves jumping or flinching when somebody touches you unexpectedly, that's the control piece. The part of you that only feels safe if you are quite literally, but often subconsciously, holding yourself together. This was definitely my story, and I've had many breakthrough moments about allowing myself to be supported over the last decade. My first was approximately six months into my entrepreneurial journey, when I was doing a program in which I was asked the simplest question, 'Do you feel supported?' And I felt the heaviness on my shoulders and started crying. I had been living my life as though no one had had my back, when it suddenly became so clear in that moment that what I'd believed wasn't true at all.

Of course, I'd had moments where I had been let down by people, people that should have known better, and done better, at least from my perspective. But I had also been wildly supported by my foster parents and the fact that I even ended up with them, people that loved me and cared for me as though I was their own, was support beyond anything that three-month-old me could have comprehended on the first night I was left in their arms and found my way into their hearts. Thinking about this as I allowed my tears to fall, I realized that the impact of my foster parents' love and support extended beyond the physical realm. It was ongoing and always would be, despite neither of them being Earth-side anymore.

Realizing this was just the beginning of a journey that I'm still on today, but it had an immediate impact on what I had the capacity to receive. Optimal receiving happens when we're open and receptive, not closed and contracted. So, however well you have done up until this point, know that there's so much more when you are willing to let people in.

~ Q&A ~

Q: I'm designing a new course to sell and I recognize that I'm in the struggle vibe. Can you help me tap into the receiving vibe more? I think that it's such a different way of looking at everything that I'm not fully in the possibility that it's there for me.

A: This question centers on remembering your unique greatness and being willing to ask for support. What I do, before I even put pen to paper, is to really connect with who I am, what it is that I desire to deliver, and the transformation that people are going to receive when they choose to go all in with me. In remembering that there is no one on the planet that can deliver what I am about to deliver in the way that I am going to deliver it, in leaning into my unique expression, the energy of everything I am about to do and touch shifts into excitement and the eager anticipation of being about to share. This is different from 'push energy'; this is about barely being able to contain myself because of what I know my soon-to-be clients are about to experience. There is no desperation or 'need-to/got-to' energy. I'm in pure desire and excitement mode.

How do you get there? Step one: Connect with the transformation and prepare for what is going to be a truly one-of-a-kind transmission that is coming from you. Then, ask yourself what you could release, let go of, or delegate in order to create more space for you to focus on your specific zone of genius. Where's the first place you could allow yourself to be supported? Remember, this doesn't mean that you have to delegate everything. This is a process; it always starts with one thing and then continues to grow. So, where are you willing to do things differently this time and let something go so that you can align your actions with the bigger vision that you are creating for yourself?

Faith + Action = Miracles

Chapter 9

Pillar of Infinite Support – Universal Knowing

I don't think you'd be reading this book if you weren't interested in the question, 'What is this life? What's the point of this journey?'

It's my belief that the point of this journey is to remember and connect with our limitless and unbridled potential. To remember that every living thing on this planet is connected and is an individuated expression of the original Source energy; you might call it God, Universal Intelligence, the Universe – please use whatever feels most aligned to you. From this perspective, the magic that we are knows no bounds and the point of this journey is simply to remember that.

And because it's the same Source energy that runs through all things, I've heard people talk about this using the metaphor of a golden thread, which I think is beautiful. Others simply call it 'consciousness.' Whatever your preference is, know that this is what I am referring to when I say that there is no separation. This golden thread binds us all to each other and all things, irrespective of race, religion, social background, or environmental context. This golden thread not only contains the building blocks of life but connects us to the wisdom of the Universe and all of its intelligence.

It's interesting when you look at some of the most famous scientists and philosophers of our time: the origins of concepts and wisdom that have stood the test of time didn't come to people when they were trying to work things out, but when they were relaxed, or dreaming. The greatest artists in the world talk about the brain switching off and their creations coming through them as though they were a conduit for the creation. Mozart creating symphonies at eight years old. Some might say he was a genius; others might say he was just 'tapped in' to this golden thread.

Part of your journey to receiving infinitely more is to choose to remember that you have access to this wisdom, too. We all do. And the beauty of this remembering is that when we tune in to it, the idea that we're ever truly alone or unsupported dissolves. The wisdom of life that is running through you can be your greatest guide and teacher if you allow it. It's always present and you are never alone.

When I walk, you walk.
Every step I take, you take.

Constant support

Once you choose to know this, you can immediately access a whole different level of trust. Over the last 25 years, the level of trust I have in myself, combined with the knowledge and trust that I'm part of something much bigger than myself, has little by little not only transformed my life but increased my level of receiving beyond recognition. And yet, I still forget this knowing hundreds of times a day. What this looks like is stress, worrying about the future, overthinking, trying to over-engineer situations, trying to anticipate how everyone else is going to think or respond, and an inability to simply be present with what is happening in the moment.

I know you get me, and I really want you to hear me when I say, you don't need to become the next Eckhart Tolle or Gandhi in order to have the concept start to weave its magic in your life now. As I've said before, the gift that is Infinite Receiving is a lifetime's journey. It's not about needing to get it right, or have it be perfect in order for you to increase your capacity to receive now. That's the beauty of it.

What does this look like in practical terms? In my work today, I travel around the world to give talks, I host three-day seminars, and deliver classes and workshops online. I actually started delivering presentations over 20 years ago when I worked in advertising sales, but back then my process for creation and preparation looked a lot different to the way it does now. Back then I'd spend hours and hours learning my whole presentation – adopting the attitude, 'fail to prepare and prepare to fail.' And what I did worked. I'd learn every slide, get clear on every facial expression, intonation, everything, and I'd deliver it like a stand-up comedian, trying to look as if it was all effortless. Even the jokes I made were designed to look and sound as though I had just made them up on the spot. Creating a 60-minute presentation took days of work.

Now a 60-minute presentation will take me 15–30 minutes to prepare – depending on the material, of course. How? Once again I have Regan Hillyer to thank. I'd watch her present the most incredible workshops for days – with no notes! When I'd ask her how she remembered everything she was going to say, she would blow my mind when she would tell me that she hadn't prepared like I used to. She would go into the space that she was presenting, feel into the energy of the group, and then deliver what she felt was going to be of the highest benefit to everyone. What?! This sounded like potential career suicide for me. There was no way that I was willing to just trust that I wasn't going to fall flat on my face. And I resisted, and resisted, and resisted until my first live and in-person three-day event.

I was going to be on stage for around 30 hours over the period of three days straight. And there was no way on this earth that I could have prepared for that event like I used to prepare for presentations in the past; there weren't enough hours in my life to do that and so I was forced into choosing trust. Of course, I had an outline of what I was going to be saying, you can't just wing 30 hours of content, but at the same time, I had a lot of space. And it was then that I discovered what happens when you create space and – instead of allowing your brain to fill it with looping projections into the future or being on the endless merry-go-round of the past – you use the space to just listen to the space guiding you into how it gets to be filled. This was a scary concept to run with, but I wasn't sure what else I could do except go with it, so I did. I had to trust.

There is one other important thing to say here: In my experience, this doesn't work if you're teaching or sharing something you don't know very well. The reason that this 'formula' is able to work for Regan and myself is because we are teaching what we are living. Our lives and experiences are the content. So, as long as I have a clear intention and some bullet points on the objective of the section – which of course can change in the moment – I know what examples and stories to draw on, because it's my experience.

That weekend was a seminal one for me, for more than one reason. First off, I realized that being on stage in that way, coaching, sharing, and teaching with incredible humans wanting to do incredible things in their lives and in their businesses is my happy place. I had never felt more alive, more activated, more *on* purpose, more in my work than at that event. I'd had tasters of this feeling before, but here everything fell into place. What I saw was that my brain was limited in what it thought was possible for me when it was trying to control everything. What I experienced in practice was that when I led through the heart, choosing trust, coming at it from a place of deep, deep presence, not only was I going to be all right, the guests would have a phenomenal time and there would be breakthrough after breakthrough, after breakthrough. That is what that weekend was and so much more. But also, from a financial perspective, my first three-day event was mind-blowing as I made over £270k in sales.

I was in flow. I felt connected to both myself *and* something bigger, and all the thoughts, feelings, stories, and beliefs that often prevent me from accessing that state of being just dissipated every time I stepped on that stage. If you can, imagine yourself, your body, as a conduit or a channel for Source energy. This is how it feels when I'm in this state of being, which I call 'being in flow.' It's a feeling that can only really be accessed through being deeply present. The more present you are, the easier it will be for you to connect or be aware of that ever-present Source energy. Your job is to notice the things, stories, and thoughts that stop you from being present. Ultimately, you want to clear as many of those things as possible, because the clearer your channel is, the easier it is for you to tune in. The more tuned in you are, the easier life tends to flow in the good times, and the more adept you become at being able to navigate the challenging times.

To be clear, being tapped into Universal wisdom, support, and intelligence doesn't stop bad things or challenging things happening to you. You can't become a 'good enough' student of the work to avoid challenge, because challenge is part of the human experience. But when you are tuned in, it's easier to see the challenge for what it is, which is simply a moment in time that you always have the opportunity to receive something from, whether it's a teaching, resilience, an idea, or a new level of tolerance. There's always something for you to receive for yourself when you are willing to consciously engage with the experience.

The other added benefit of engaging is that it feels really good in your body. You can relax more. You see more of the beauty that is life right in front of you, reflected in the eyes and the hearts of your fellow humans; you see it and feel it in the nature and animals that surround you. You also feel it in the stillness and the quiet. And it feels exquisite.

Let's try this breathing exercise, which you'll also find as an audio version in the *Empower You Unlimited Audio* app (search 'Meditations for Infinite Receiving').

Transformational Tools

Close your eyes, if it's good and safe for you to do so, and just breathe. Focus your attention on the heart space. Notice the gentle rising and falling of the chest as you gently inhale and exhale. And as you continue breathing, making the exhalation slightly longer than the inhalation, I invite you to just allow any thoughts you have to pass right on through, choosing to avoid diving into any of them, and to keep bringing your attention back to the heart space.

As you continue breathing, I want you to imagine a light in the center of your chest. See the white light getting bigger with each inhalation, and with every exhalation, allowing the white light to diffuse until that light is filling every cell in your chest, and then allow it to move all around your body, so your entire body is filled with light. Then allow your light to move beyond the barriers of your skin so you are completely surrounded by it. As you continue to breathe, with every inhalation the light getting bigger and with every exhalation allowing your light to fill the space in which you are sitting, notice how your body feels.

Write down in your journal what you have noticed.

Clearing the channel

In the spiritual world, people talk about *needing* a clear channel in order to be able to connect with Source. My belief is that your connection with Source is ever-present. I have had just as many spiritual and profound experiences during phases when I have consumed alcohol, eaten meat, and not been meditating daily as I have when I've done the reverse. What I instinctively know to be true, and what was confirmed when I started training for a sex, love, and relationship certification with my friend and mentor Layla Martin, who teaches through a Tantric philosophy lens, is that everything gets to be a portal to the Divine, without exception. Your intention to connect is the most potent and powerful tool at your disposal. This idea that you need to be 'good enough' to feel it comes from religious programing that says that you can 'good' your way into heaven, which isn't helpful at all. Universal energy doesn't discriminate, it runs through us all and, regardless of how 'good' or 'bad' a person is, they can connect to that energy in an instant. Your connection can't be broken. I do think, though, that it can be easier to remember that when you're not distracted by brain fog or your energy isn't already being used to contain old, outdated stories and beliefs that you no longer need to hold on to.

Often when people read my words or listen to my videos, they comment on the awareness they have of energy moving or congregating in the body. I'm not doing anything to make this happen. That is just you becoming consciously aware of your connection to your life force energy, Source energy. It's always there, always present, it's just that most of the time you're not being intentional when it comes to noticing it, feeling it, or tuning into it. So, rather than worrying about needing to do anything in order to be connected, outside of using your intention and noticing, my recommendation is to just do things that make you, your mind, and your body feel good. Let go of the things that don't feeling nourishing, because when you're not feeling good because of how you're treating yourself, it makes it way easier to be distracted from the magic that is serving you well. What's good for me is going to be different for you, but when you give me musical dance breaks, breath work, less alcohol than when I was 20, long walks by the sea, and meditation, I definitely tend to feel my connection more. If you don't already know what feels great for you, commit to finding out and be prepared for those things to change depending on what season of life you are in. Nourish yourself and appreciate the blessing that is your physical being in all its glory and perceived imperfection. Get intentional about being with yourself and what feels nourishing – and notice that 'good' isn't always nourishing. This is your invitation to take the opportunity to receive endless and limitless feedback from yourself. That's pretty amazing!

Transformational Tools

I do the following exercises and ask the following questions of myself on an ongoing basis; they're the tools that I use to help myself to tune in. I invite you to try them for yourself.

Look at where the places are in your life right now where you know that there are more opportunities for you to be supported. Notice any places where you observe yourself thinking that you should be able to cope already, or other people can do it, why can't you? As you write out this list, allow it to be the highest vision of support you have for yourself and give yourself permission over time to be the person who's willing to ask for guidance on who you get to choose to be, and then what you have to do to be an energetic match for what you desire.

Next, set the intention that you are creating a life where you are infinitely supported in all areas. The more support that you allow, the less you do, the more you receive. And thirdly, ask yourself, 'What gets to shift in this area for me to allow more support?'

Notice any areas where you are currently not in trust; where you're forcing and pushing your way through in order to guarantee a specific result. Tune in and ask yourself: How would you approach things differently if you were truly in trust?

If you're not a writer and you don't feel comfortable writing in your journal, then you can always use your phone to record your reflections into voice notes.

For me, journaling is a powerful tool and I use it in a number of different ways. Sometimes, I will ask a question and then self-coach myself through the answer. Other times, I will free write without filtering, without thinking, just allowing the new information to come through.

Anyone who is familiar with Julia Cameron's wonderful book *The Artist's Way* will know that this technique is called Morning Pages.

She recommends that you write freestyle for three pages every morning to see what comes up. I used to do that a lot and I think it's super helpful for tuning into the subconscious thoughts and beliefs to bring them to the surface.

I also use journaling to tune in to my own inner voice, my inner guidance, my own higher self. So, through a stream-of-consciousness journaling, perhaps I'll notice a problem or stress that I'm carrying with me. I'll then pause writing to 'tune in'; what I mean by that is I connect with the part of me that goes beyond the intellect of the mind. I want to connect with the energetic thread of Universal knowing that runs through me and all things. I bring my attention to my breath, anchoring myself to the present moment and bringing heightened awareness to my body, and at that point, I'll ask myself a question, such as: 'Is this true?' Or, 'If I was whole, complete, and enough, what would I know to be true about this situation? What am I not seeing about this situation?'

From that place, I just write, and I see what comes through. It's such a simple process that takes me beyond what my mind 'knows.' I'm tuned into Universal knowing. How do I know? Often, the answers that come through are profound, but wildly simple. My mind frequently wants to complicate what it sees as 'the problem.' The minute I start thinking, or analyzing, or arguing with what's coming through, I know that my conscious mind is active again and looking for ways to protect me from doing something that it perceives to be unsafe. If I'm critically thinking or anticipating what the answer should be, I'm not in the zone. I'm in my head.

Try it and see how you get on. While I have nothing against rituals – they can be extremely powerful activators – I want you to know that you don't have to do anything externally to connect with the Universal Intelligence that is ever-present and able to guide and support you. You don't need to be lighting sage sticks and meditating for an hour at a time to connect with it. You can if you feel like doing that; I do like doing that, but that's not been my practice in terms of bringing my awareness to that wider connection.

And if you trust that every step and every lesson is guiding you to where you need to be for the next phase in your story, the next chapter in the book, then there are no wrong steps – or even, the 'wrong' steps are ultimately right. You needed to make the mistake in order to receive the lesson. It's super helpful to remember this when you get stuck in your head, over-thinking the next little step so much that all forward momentum stops, as you stop moving and start creating by default from a place of confusion and fear as opposed to consciously creating what you desire. And please don't misunderstand me, there have definitely been times in my life where pausing has been necessary to feel into what's coming next, but the feeling of a pause is different from being stuck. While a pause can still feel uncomfortable if, like me, your natural tendency is to *do*, there's a sense of allowing, and knowing, and a feeling that you're on the edge of something that is in its gestation period, and the only thing you can do is pause while it's being developed.

The best comparison I have is growing a human, being pregnant. When we're what is commonly known as 'stuck,' that's a whole different frequency, where we choose waiting to avoid making the wrong decision. In one mode we're in the part of creation that happens before we take conscious and aligned action to take us toward what it is we're creating, and in the other mode we're taking a defensive or protective standpoint, where the number-one focus is making the right decision or avoiding the wrong one. It's a completely different experience. However, when you allow yourself to come back to knowing that you are whole, complete, and enough in any and all ways, you release the pressure. And that creates freedom both in the mind and for the body for you to take the next step.

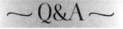

Q: I'm in the zone and in a state of flow right now and it's amazing, but my partner just doesn't get it and doesn't understand what I'm talking about. How do we coexist? How do I bring them along for the journey? I guess what I'm saying is that people in the real world don't get it, and when they come into my space, I feel the need to either push them to understand or to push them away in order to keep the integrity of my energy.

A: No one really loves the answer to this question, but here it is anyway. You have to do you. It's not your job to even try to take anyone along for the journey and the more you try, the more resistance you'll run into most times. What I've found to be true – and I speak this from the perspective of someone who was in a relationship for 15 years and now has a successful co-parenting relationship – is that the best way to get someone to want to be interested in what you are doing, and potentially understand how what you are doing could be great for them too, is for them to see you living it, not just talking about it. They also need to feel that you're not judging *them* for not living it. Let them experience you being the model for what it is that you are committing to, rather than being the mirror for their confusion or potential fear about the changes that they are witnessing in you. Let them feel the ripple effect of your increased level of self-love, see you being kinder to yourself and to others, see you setting intentions and following through, and notice you consciously creating the things that you once talked about wanting. Most of the parenting books I've ever read all say the same thing; children don't do what you tell them, they emulate what they see. And this is frequently true for the people that we love and are the closest to in life.

The truth is that it can be really challenging when a partner or the people who feel that they know you best see you changing; often the thought is, 'What's my role in this new person's life? Are they still going to love me? What about the things we used to do? Why doesn't any of that feel good enough anymore?' There's a huge internal shift happening and, depending on how fearful or threatened your loved one feels, it's not unusual for them to not only not be interested in your journey but to actively push back against it. This isn't their fault. It happens frequently and, as frustrating as it might feel, it's the perfect opportunity for you to practice noticing how you feel, transmuting those emotions where necessary, and to demonstrate how you are growing in all ways.

When you stay committed in this way, choosing to love and accept your partner anyway and finding spaces where you can have the conversations and support you are looking for and are worthy of, one of two things tends to happen. Your partner, off their own bat, will either decide that they want to know more and will start asking you questions and wanting to get involved, or they won't. And if they don't, over time you ultimately both have to decide whether that's a deal-breaker or not. But long before you get to that stage, you have to look at what it is that it's going to take for you to be able to practice what you preach – which is tough! But you've got this, I know you have.

Faith + Action = Miracles

Chapter 10

Pillar of Infinite Love – Love Is the Strongest Medicine

If I was allowed a favorite pillar, this would be it. I LOVE talking about the Love Pillar, because whenever I get into this topic, I feel a whole new level of activation for myself, as well as seeing the amazing effects on everyone I come into contact with (and that now includes you, by the way!) For me, everything drops down to a deeper level. The way this chapter is going to work is: I'm going to share with you some of the biggest things that I've observed blocking people from being an open conduit for love, the ultimate healing medicine; what it means to lead with love in business; and how you can open yourself up to a s***load more love in your own life. Who doesn't want that?

I consider myself to be loving, kind, and caring, and I surround myself with individuals who reflect the same qualities. People who I wouldn't hesitate to describe as heart-centered. We all care, we all want to make a positive difference to the people who are in our lives, to make a difference to the people whose lives we touch through our work. We fully understand that love is the strongest medicine. But being heart-centered is not the same as living your life with your heart open.

I don't remember where it first found me, but a message that has stuck to my heart like one of my children's faces is that I get to choose whether I am going to act from love or fear. The root of all actions, the root of everything, will be based on either one or the other. Most of us, most of the time, are coming from a place of fear because we live our lives from the frequency of low-level anxiety. This means that we don't realize when we're not choosing to come from love, and that matters because our energetic projection out into the world impacts everyone we come into contact with, and then everyone they come into contact with. So, how you feel and how that translates out into the world absolutely matters. Does this mean that there's no space for you ever to feel bad or low? No, because to deny your full range of emotions would be to deny your humanness. However, paying attention to whether you're closing down or choosing to open your heart up consistently will change your life.

So, most of us are living our lives from a place of fear because low-level anxiety is the norm. That comes in all shapes and sizes. It might show up as impatience when your chatty neighbor wants to talk for just a little longer than you have time for. You're afraid that you're going to run out of time, so you close yourself – and your heart – off a little bit, hoping that they will feel the vibe or the disconnection and stop talking. Maybe you're writing a post that is promoting your next offer and you're afraid that you don't have the right words to help people make a decision, and so you feel stressed and anxious as you just want to get it right. You're not deliberately closing yourself off but, because you're stressed, your frequency is not attuned to love in that moment at all. Or perhaps you feel that you're tired of being let down, not just because it creates more work for you, but because it hurts your heart. So, you create a protective barrier around it in order to prevent your heart from getting hurt again. And perhaps the wounds that your heart holds are old and run deep, and the only option for you up until this point has been to shut everything down.

I get it. For basically my entire life, I have lived with a protective barrier around my heart and I know my loved ones absolutely didn't get the best of me, and when I say that I mean me in my most open-hearted, vulnerable state of being. Because I am a kind, caring, and loving person, I managed to fool everyone (including myself) into thinking that I was an open-hearted individual – but I wasn't. Heart-centered and open-hearted is not the same thing. Living open-hearted means that you're willing to take risks with your heart; you're willing to look stupid for the things and people you love and care about; you're willing to give 100 percent, not just 99 percent; you'll say to yourself AND the world that you're willing to go all in, and that is a HUGE deal. Living your life with an open heart takes a huge amount of courage, and that's why so many of us don't want to fully commit.

For many people, especially in the business world, talking about love feels very strange. I remember once being invited to speak at an event for small business owners. As per usual, I invited everyone to get up and dance with me. While this isn't the most usual way to start a talk, most people are willing to give it a go. It's a beautiful icebreaker, and an opportunity for me to connect with the audience and the audience to connect with each other as we enjoy this mini-peak experience. When doesn't it feel great to move your body after you've been stuck in your seat for hours at a time while people talk at you? This particular time, though, I had a table right at the front of the room that just didn't want to participate. While I am not a mind reader, this is what I think happened: One person felt uncomfortable and decided that they were going to 'disengage'; that this wasn't what they had come to receive, they didn't want to play the game so they didn't, and their energy impacted the person next to them, so they decided to close off, and so did the person next to *them*, and so on.

Interestingly, in response, I went to a place of fear. There was a part of me that immediately went to, 'Oh, I'm s***. I'm not good enough.' I went to a place of not loving myself and definitely not loving them. I went to the part of me that desperately wanted to prove them wrong. And then, I caught myself. What if I had nothing to prove to them, or even myself, anyway? What if I could trust the process and know that they were receiving EXACTLY what they were supposed to be receiving in that moment? And what if I could keep my heart open to them and the experience, and hold on to the knowledge that I could receive exactly what I was supposed to receive in that moment, too? And what I was receiving is this story, which is now the gift that keeps on giving as I use it as an example of how easy it is to close your heart down when you feel threatened.

They felt threatened and I felt threatened. This is the prelude to all conflict. Unless someone is willing to allow their barriers to soften, the impasse quickly becomes conflict. I chose to release my fear in the moment so that I could consciously receive. If I hadn't, my internal struggle with needing things to be different would have derailed the entire talk. Once again, it's understanding that I don't need to be Mother Teresa for this situation to morph into a portal of transformation. I wasn't in love with that table by the end of my talk but, by choosing acceptance, I was able to open my heart just a little bit more than when I looked at their disengagement as a threat to me.

There were so many lessons to be taken from the experience at that event, both for the people on that table and for me, but none was more important than the truth that Infinite Receiving is about knowing that you are at the center of all that you create. We can create chaos or we can create calm, and how dialled in to our heart space we are at any given time will frequently determine how things play out. Now, before we go any further, let's open our hearts up just a little bit more.

Transformational Tools

Take a moment and close your eyes and bring your attention to the heart space.

Take a couple of deep breaths and, as you exhale, I want you to drop a little deeper into the heart space.

If your legs are crossed, it's better to have both feet on the floor, because you want to keep the whole channel of your body open.

Notice where you're holding any tension and give yourself permission to let go just a little bit more with every exhalation.

Now, I invite you, simply with your intention, to open the heart just a little more than it is already, and just notice what shifts; the smallest or the largest of observations: perhaps you notice a change or a shift in your physical body, a shift in your emotions, or perhaps a change in your awareness and a thought you have just had. What shifts do you notice as you allow the heart to be a little more open?

It might be positive for you, or you might notice a bit of fear coming up. Any observation is valid. Don't judge it, just observe it.

Now open your eyes and jot down in your journal what you just observed.

In my experience of this heart-opening exercise, feelings can range from being a little uncomfortable and feeling exposed, to resistance, or even numbness, through to feeling calm, connected, and serene. Your full range of emotions are welcome – the beautiful thing about love is that it coexists with them all when you allow it to.

⌒ Affirmation ⌒

'I am Love. I am Exquisite. I am a Masterpiece.
I am Love.'

All Pillars entwine

If you look at the work that we've covered with the first two Pillars, namely seeing yourself in your Infinite Greatness and allowing yourself to be infinitely supported, this third portal is intrinsic to the first two. Why? Because you can't see yourself in your Infinite Greatness when your heart is closed down. Similarly, you can't allow yourself to know the support that is available to you, both practically and universally, if your heart is closed down.

The more that you open your heart, the more you'll be able to see the greatness in you and other people, the more you'll be able to allow yourself to be supported infinitely.

While the Pillars of Infinite Receiving are not linear, they do work with, support, and amplify each other. If you know that your heart has been closed down, then choosing to consciously work to open your heart is not only going to support you in giving and receiving more love, but it will also support you in knowing your greatness and allowing yourself to be even more supported.

The truth is that protection mode is our default. That is why the Love and Support Pillars are so entwined. We stop ourselves from being supported when we've been let down and it hurts. We stop our hearts from being open when we've had our heart broken, and it hurts. We don't want to feel that pain again. The first time our heart is broken, the first time our heart hurts, is the first time we start to build up our defense mechanisms.

When heartbreak has happened at a young age, the defense mechanisms that you unconsciously created as a child will often still be operating in your life, business, and relationships without you even being aware of it. And, depending on your personality, your protection mechanisms might not even be obvious to the outside world. You might present yourself as being a happy, smiley individual who loves to support others, when in fact you are not. Your ability and capacity to stop yourself from being truly vulnerable with your heart and to keep it protected is silent but masterful.

At the other end of the spectrum are those who obviously close themselves off, because they are still actively dealing with old wounds and don't feel safe to open their hearts. They will literally push people away and let them down, and might suffer from addiction, anger, rage, and depression.

Choosing to be aware of our defense mechanisms, and choosing to make that awareness matter, is a sign that the Pillar of Love is already starting to work its magic. Because, although love absolutely does have boundaries, it does create the space for empathy. Love is understanding and love is empathy.

There are many incidents in a person's past that could have caused them to close down their heart, from the seemingly insignificant to the 'big-T' trauma. Perhaps someone excluded them from the games at school or a teacher made them feel inadequate or, on the other side of the scale, they experienced grief because of a relationship ending that they weren't ready to let go of or they were abused. All of these things, and so many in between, can cause a person to want to shut down their heart.

As I've deepened my own studies into trauma, and the impact it has on peoples' lives, I've realized that there isn't a person on the planet who hasn't experienced some kind of trauma that impacts the way that they show up in the world. The forgiveness process that I shared in the Pillar of Support chapters is really helpful when it comes to moving beyond these experiences that have kept us shut down. However, it's important to say that if there are times when it feels too much for you to work through your experiences on your own, it's time to reach out and seek outside support. Trauma has such a wide spectrum.

The more that you open your heart, the more you'll be able to see the greatness in you and other people.

Full expression

To be in the space of receiving infinitely, you have to be willing to be all of yourself, to be in your fullness, and part of that fullness is the full expression of the heart's experience. So, if your default behavior is protection, my invitation to you is vulnerability.

Vulnerability goes against playing it safe. Vulnerability goes against trying to avoid looking stupid. It goes against trying to anticipate the next 100 steps: 'If I do this, maybe this will happen. If I do that, maybe that will happen.' Vulnerability is the opposite of playing chess with yourself or trying to mitigate the risk. It's the opposite of copying other people; so much of the desire to emulate comes from the idea, 'If I do it like this successful person, I'm going to avoid having my heart broken because I'll be getting it right, too.'

Vulnerability is the opposite of trying to stop people from seeing the real version of you. And I get it. Why do we want to put ourselves in the position of saying, 'This is me,' and have people reject us? Why would anybody want that?

Yet, what I'm inviting you to do is to make a conscious decision to go against everything that feels safe and to say, 'This is me' in work, in life, and in relationships. Gah! And as scary as that might sound – and I think it should sound a little scary – when you commit to this level of vulnerability, you'll experience more of life and more of yourself. You'll experience yourself in all your glory, in all your magic, holding no bits of yourself back.

Experiencing all of your magic comes with the good, the bad, and the ugly. Which is why it's so important to surround yourself with a community that treats you with a huge amount of compassion, love, and empathy. As you give yourself permission to be supported, seen, and loved for all that you are, it makes it easier for you to support, see, and love the people in your life and business for all that they are. You might not agree with everything that a person says or does, but you can still see their greatness.

When we try to protect ourselves and make ourselves more palatable to others, we actually limit our capacity to receive.

Taking a risk

Choosing vulnerability is risky. What you're actually saying is, 'I will bare my heart to you in the shape of my hopes, my dreams, and my desires, and I realize that I might not always get exactly what I want when I want it in return.' But, as an Infinite Receiver, I know that I will always be receiving something, so I am willing to do the thing anyway and risk my heart being smashed into a thousand pieces.

That isn't an easy thing to opt in to, but if you really want to play the game of Infinite Receiving the way that I'm inviting you to play it (i.e., to go beyond the surface), that is the risk I'm asking you to take.

What that risk looks like on a practical level is you being willing to ask yourself:

- What is it that I want to say?

- What is my truth?

- Am I living a life and running a business that lights me up?

- What's the impact that I truly desire to make?

- Am I willing to go all in on that, even if nobody freaking gets it?

My belief is that when we're living in our fullest alignment, there will always be at least one person who's a match for the truth that is coming from within us, because that truth is really coming from Universal Intelligence. I don't believe that we're given anything that is not supposed to connect and make a difference to at least one person.

And when you're living in your fullest alignment and taking that risk, your heart is open and its magic is at its most potent. And when the heart's magic is at its most potent, you are at your most potent, and your presence, your being, and (when you want to use them) your words hold the most power.

I like to think of the heart as both a conduit for the frequency of love and a generator. While this isn't strictly accurate, because energy cannot be created or destroyed, we do have the capacity to increase the amount of love in our lives through choosing to allow love to flow through us; allowing it to pour into both ourselves and others.

As a mum, I was fearful that I wouldn't be able to love another child as much as I did my first, but what I learned was that my heart expanded with every child, allowing more and more love to flow through with each child. That was all the evidence that I needed.

Love in business

I applied the knowledge that the more I'm able to operate from a field of love, the more I receive back to my business. Don't believe me? I get it: Love isn't necessarily the most popular subject when it comes to business, it feels a bit fluffy. When it comes to the money and the management of multi-million pound corporations, or companies that are barely able to make ends meet, is there even a place for love? In both my world and the real world, the answer is, yes.

Love is at the heart of some of the most successful personal brands that I've worked with over the last few years; the type of brand where you are able to get under the hood of what they are actually doing. It's there that I have spent time with my favorite and most successful mentors. These people love not just the lives that they are living, they love the lives that they are touching. They love their clients, and the people who surround them and support them, but they also have a vision for a better world that is ever-present.

When I visited Necker Island in 2022, I was blown away by the level of intimacy that my mentor Sir Richard Branson had with his team members. He knew every single one of the 80 staff members by name and, aged 71 at the time, that was pretty impressive. When he talked about his personal vision, which was to see a world without war, and he shared some of his attempts throughout the years to use his influence for good on that front, the overwhelming impression that I was left with (despite some of the controversies that I had read about in the press) was that he cared about leaving the world a better place. And he cared about you feeling seen and felt by him.

In business, you will have a completely different energy field if you are deeply connected to how your product or program is going to change your next client's life, compared to if you are focused solely on money. A potential client is going to read your social media posts completely differently when you share something from the heart that is designed to support them in seeing the world differently, as opposed to when you have agonized over every word, trying to guarantee that you make the sale. One way is you-focused, the other way is people-focused. The more you care, the more you love, the more people feel it in both the short and long term, the more it will make a difference.

At the same time, loving your work and your people doesn't mean over-working, over-giving or not having boundaries. It's not, 'Let me give you everything to prove how much I love you.' It's not about under-charging or not telling the truth in order to save someone's feelings. It's being willing to take a stand for the transformation you know is possible and choosing to come from that place first, *especially* when you could do with the money.

> The magic of the heart is at its most potent when it is open. When the heart is at its most potent, you are at your most potent; your power, your presence, and your words hold the most power.

Love can't be turned off

I like to think of the cycle of love as the infinity loop, a figure of eight, and you are right in the center of it. Although you are not giving with any expectation of receiving from the same source, what has been proven to be true time and time again is, the more love you give out, the more you receive; the more you receive, the more you can give out. It's you in the center, and the only time that you can't feel the flow is when you close your heart down.

The beautiful thing is that you can't turn the frequency of love off. Even when you close or restrict your heart's capacity to receive, love is still all around you and your heart is always a conduit for it. Your heart always has the capacity to receive more love and to send more out.

Letting Love in

So, how do we consciously and consistently choose to open our heart more, aside from choosing to be more vulnerable?

This invitation is a simple and powerful one. I want you to ask yourself as many times a day as you can remember (a great activation point could be when you are starting a new activity), 'Can I open my heart just a little more right now?' Or, 'Is my heart open?' Take two minutes to consciously bring your awareness to your heart and open it, just as we did at the start of this chapter, and you'll be amazed at how it changes your experience of everything, including yourself, as you become a conduit for more and more love. As you give more, you receive more – infinitely.

Now, you may have noticed that this heart-opening exercise brought up some fear, some tightness, some discomfort perhaps. The reason those feelings may arise is that, as we discussed, it can feel viscerally unsafe to have your heart open.

What I want to say to you is that being vulnerable *is* unsafe. You're not being weird if it feels uncomfortable. In opening your heart, you are going against the programming that you have created your whole life to keep you protected. But you have to ask yourself, 'What is the game that I desire to play? The one where I keep myself safe, so I don't get my heart smashed into a thousand pieces, but with no chance of ever experiencing the full richness of myself and what life has to offer? Or the one where I know that potentially my heart might get smashed, but I am living a life beyond what I thought was possible because I allowed myself to go all in?' I mean, you're here for a reason, right?

What I'm talking about is exponentially increasing your quality of life across every single area, while knowing that the more love you allow in and become a conduit for, the more attractive in every possible way you become.

Again, being a portal for love doesn't protect you from bad things happening. But, it does equip you with the power of empathy; it makes forgiveness easier and, most importantly, it keeps you open to the goodness and abundance that is always flowing even when 'bad' stuff is happening, too. So, the commitment you're making to yourself is to consistently ask yourself, 'Is my heart open?' and to bring your awareness to shifting it until it becomes muscle memory. With this exercise, you're promising to do your workouts in Soul Gym multiple times a day but, as with any muscle, the more you use it, the stronger it becomes and the more your muscle memory kicks in.

Transformational Tools

So, to close this chapter, I invite you to go into the coming days with the intention of having your heart open. Check in with yourself as many times a day as possible, and then share in your journal what differences you notice.

If you notice that you've got to the end of the day without even once asking yourself, 'Is my heart open?' then I want you to reflect on how you felt during the day: what type of day have you had? Write down what you have observed in your journal without any judgment. Maybe you had an incredible day, maybe you didn't; all is welcome, your job is just to notice.

Then, before you go to sleep, set a very clear intention to remember to wake up and bring your awareness to opening up your heart. And keep coming back to the question, 'Is my heart open?' If you find yourself in need of a little assistance, use your alarm on your phone to set little reminders throughout the day to get you into a groove.

In this way, you can recognize what it feels like when you are consciously opening your heart and when something happens and you get knocked out of it, and then look at the contrast.

~ Q&A ~

Q1: *I find myself feeling overwhelmed by my emotions. In truth, I'm tired of feeling all my emotions. How can I live in my fullness when I feel like this?*

A: You're feeling overwhelmed because you haven't learned to release the emotions that are no longer serving you once you've extracted the lesson.

You may feel like you are in the middle of a tidal wave of emotion; your emotions have completely taken you over and you don't know what to do with them. Unless you are in an extreme trauma response (if this is the case, then it is time to reach out for outside support), what is usually happening is that the story, and the meaning that you have given to the story, have gotten so big that the emotions have expanded to match it. In situations like this, go back to the simplicity of the E in Motion Tool (p.80), consciously releasing the story and engaging solely with the emotion to re-empower yourself. Then, you're choosing the experience, rather than it overwhelming you. You'll experience the same release with the support of an Infinite Receiving Coach.

You get to remember that your emotions are signposts for the things you need to learn or deal with. When you're feeling angry, that anger has a purpose. So, I invite you to ask the question, 'What do I need to see, hear, or remember that I am not right now, that this anger (sadness, frustration, resentment) wants to share with me?' It's often useful to do this in a journal before you start with the E in Motion Tool. Once you learn what it is that the emotion wants to reveal to you, you then get to transmute what's left.

Q2: While I'm focusing on a specific area that I want to manifest or receive in, I feel like there's other stuff I'm not focusing on so much. (For me, it's often the Love portal I neglect.) Sometimes, it feels like I'm not expanding my capacity in all areas of my life, because I don't have the ability to. What are your thoughts on this?

A: The energy of this question is on the frequency of scarcity. Like, 'If I don't put all my attention on to a thing, then I'm not going to manifest it. If I put my attention here, then I'm not manifesting over there.' From that place, it makes it way more challenging to receive what it is you want, because you're already telling yourself that it's not possible. So, you get to release the story that unless your mind is on the thing, you're not going to be able to receive it.

I want you to reframe your question as, 'Who am I being when I am receiving all that I desire in every area?' I want you to think about who you are on a day-to-day basis. How do you organize your time? What type of things do you say yes to? What type of things do you say no to? What new beliefs do you need to hold? What old beliefs do you choose to release? Answer all of these questions from the place of having received all that you desire already.

Release the timelines and continue to keep connecting with the feelings and the knowing that your vision is already done. Then, take the action in alignment with that knowing.

Faith + Action = Miracles

Chapter 11

Pillar of Infinite Conscious Creation - Stepping into Co-creation

Everything that we've covered in the last three Pillars has been layering us up and leading us to what we're going to be covering in this chapter: namely, Infinite Conscious Creation, the fourth and final Pillar.

So, let's start as we always do with a question, and I want you to be as honest as possible when you answer: Over the past week or so, on a scale of 1 to 10, how much time have you spent consciously living your life from the place of knowing your greatness? Write in your journal the scores on the doors – you can do it as a percentage if you prefer.

When I reflected on that question for myself, I was surprised by my answer. I had enjoyed a really good weekend ahead of sitting down to write this chapter. It was super chilled. The kids were at their dad's. I'd eaten well, been for long beach walks, watched rom-coms – a really good weekend. But, honestly, I'd probably only operated from that place of knowing my greatness for less than 10 percent of the weekend. As I started writing, though, and brought my awareness to how I feel when I am choosing my greatness, I felt the difference in both my mind and my body immediately.

My point? Be mindful. If you've been fully on it and aware, that's brilliant. If, like me, you haven't, don't beat yourself up, because as I have just acknowledged, I definitely forget to be in awe of this planet and my place on it. When we are building up that muscle and we don't intentionally choose to remember our greatness, it's easy to slip back into old ways of being. So, when you realize that you're slipping, it's an invitation to shift your focus and allow the energy to change again.

What I want to reiterate is that even being in the conversation, either through the words in this book or with the people in your life, will remind you of your greatness. And as soon as your bring your attention there, you create an opportunity for a shift in your energy back into alignment with knowing your greatness.

In the same vein, answer me this: In recent weeks, when you've noticed that you've needed help in your life, have you asked for support? And how much time have you spent knowing that you are in connection with Universal support? Again, jot down a mark out of 10 or a percentage in your journal.

Just to remind you, when you're tapped into that knowing that you are universally supported, there's a lightness; you're not so stressed or worried about all the things that feel beyond your control.

You're not so much in your head. That's how you know whether you've been in connection with Universal support.

And how have you got on with keeping your heart open? When you think about your activities since you last picked up this book, how much intention, energy, and awareness were you able to bring to your heart being open? Write down your score out of 10.

A gentle reminder: When you answer these questions, be mindful that you're not berating yourself over your answers – even if there's part of you that wants to have remembered more. Being able to consciously receive starts with your awareness. And you are definitely aware now. So, wherever you are, you're on the right path.

> *Co-creation, the Infinite Receiving way,*
> *is about knowing that you are whole, and*
> *worthy, and complete right now, and anything*
> *you decide to add is just garnish.*

Creating from fullness

The reason that we looked at the Pillars of Infinite Greatness, Support, and Love before the Pillar of Infinite Co-creation is because I wanted you to understand that you are creating from a place of being a walking, talking miracle. Nothing that you get or achieve externally can add to who you are at your core, because you are whole and complete already. From this place, everything you decide to add is simply garnish, sprinkles on top of an already magnificent cake. This is why it won't work if you are creating or trying to manifest to fill a gap within yourself. Because once you get the thing that you want, you won't feel satiated.

Knowing that you are a miracle is the work of a lifetime, but the most beautiful thing about this work is that you when you know it, you'll feel changes in your life instantaneously. You don't need to be perfect or change everything, you just need to shift your awareness to feel the differences internally, and then it's simply about how frequently you can remember to come back to that awareness. The more consistent that you are, the quicker you will notice that things are changing externally for you, too. That's how you can change unconscious co-creation to conscious co-creation.

I could just as easily have asked you at the start of the chapter, 'How frequently have you felt triggered recently?' or, 'How frequently have you felt fear?' or, 'How frequently have you felt angry or pissed off?' It's not that you're never going to feel triggered. It's not that you're supposed to never feel angry, or never feel pissed off. It's about how long you stay in those places for and how quickly you extract the lesson that will tell you where you are in relation to this work.

Remember that you are manifesting all of the time, you are receiving all the time – the only difference now is that you are choosing to be more deliberate about it.

As you continue to strengthen your Infinite Receiving muscles, and your inner confidence grows, you get to ask yourself, 'How much can I enjoy and celebrate myself, and my life, now?' And you'll know that you are able to enjoy and celebrate it not just on an intellectual level, but in your heart and in your body; feeling it in every cell of your being. This happens with commitment to remembering, continually bringing yourself back to the Pillars, and recalibrating again and again.

A stable, energetic foundation

I can't stress enough that this book is not supposed to be a one-time read. Reconnecting with just one thing daily and remembering to implement it is the thing that will change your entire experience of both your life and the way you manifest. Know that wherever you are on the journey, there is always an opportunity to go deeper.

What you're looking to do is to create a stable, energetic foundation. The more stable the foundation, the easier it is for you to consciously create the material things that you desire. Here's how:

Step 1: Asking 'What do I want?'

The first step to consciously creating what it is that you want is answering the question that I've been asking you since the beginning of the book: 'What do you want?'

The biggest mistake that I see people making is not knowing, owning, or claiming what it is that they truly desire. Or, frequently, they focus on 'the garnish' rather than 'the meat' of the heart.

Now, don't get me wrong, there's nothing wrong with wanting the garnish – the money, holidays, luxury everything. And the idea that it's 'not spiritual' to want the car you want is inaccurate, especially when you've been doing the work that I have outlined. You can want the car because it's simply your preference, rather than using it as a marker to prove how worthy you really are.

But what *is* true is that when you know that this stuff is just garnish, you'll find it easier to not get distracted by it, creating more space and time for you to discover your soul's true work and mission. You'll access the type of manifestation that leaves you looking at your legacy and, most importantly, how you created it with the deepest sense of fulfillment.

So, instead of asking, 'What do I want?' you could ask: 'What does my soul want for me? What does my soul want for me today?' Ideally, you'll ask yourself this question when you have some space and quiet (the beginning of every day is a particularly good time), and I invite you to just listen for the answer and write down whatever comes up for you in your journal.

You might feel surprised, it might be more of an 'of course, this is what I want,' or it might feel scary. The invitation is to remember that you are whole, complete, and enough right now. And what you accomplish in your life will never make you more or less worthy.

But, at the same time, you were born to create and your potential for creation is limitless. So, why not? Why not listen to what your soul desires for you, as opposed to what your ego says that you should want, and then play. Play with becoming the person who lives in accordance with your soul.

If your soul desire is the main course and
your material desire is the dessert, don't skip your
main course just because you love the dessert.

Step 2: Choosing to know that the fully formed answer to your desire is already in existence

We talked about the Law of Conservation right at the beginning of the book, which refers to the fact that energy cannot be created or destroyed. This means that all of the thoughts that ever have been and ever will be are just energy that exists in this vast and infinite Universe already, floating around as untapped potential. The moment we align to the thought, or have the thought, we start the conscious creation process.

Many people then ask, 'How do I do that?' and immediately get stuck there. Turn back to everything we talked about in the Wealth Consciousness chapters: You don't have to know the 'how.' You can feel safe in the knowledge that the answer to the 'how' is out there, because the solution to every single problem is already in existence according to the Law of Conservation. Your job is to reduce the amount of time it takes for you to become an energetic match for the solution by focusing on the WHO you need to be for you to be able to see the answer.

Step 3: Who do you need to become?

This is the identity piece. This is what you have been learning and implementing since the beginning of the book.

This is the part where you look at all the stories and beliefs that don't support the manifestation you're aligning to, and let them go. If you want to create a multiple seven-figure business, for example, but you believe that there are already not enough hours in the day to create what it is that you want to create and you will need to sacrifice your health, your friends, or things that are important to you, you will absolutely block yourself from becoming the person who has what your soul desires for you.

So, as we did in the Creating Wealth chapter, write down all the reasons that you cannot create your manifestation. And then, one by one, ask yourself what you would believe to be true if you were the person who had what you wanted and had created it in a way that aligned with your values. What would you need to see, know, or believe instead?

For example:

- 'The more money I earn, the less I have to work.'

- 'I have an incredible team who support me in all that I do.'

- 'It is safe for me to earn more than ever before.'

- 'The more impact I make, the more time I get to spend with my family.'

Then, for each of these new stories, ask yourself who you need to become for it to be true:

- To earn more money for less work, I need to be the person that has a business model that makes it true. What would need to shift or change in my business model for me to create that reality?

- If I have an incredible team, then I will need to be an incredible boss. What makes a person an incredible boss?

And so, story by story, you will be mapping out your new belief and identity system.

Believe it or not, it's at this stage that many people drop out of the game, because they are not seeing their external reality shift quickly enough. I get it. This is the toughest part of the process. Keep the faith and choose to move forward with certainty.

Transformational Tools

There are a couple of ways to become more certain about what you are manifesting that are going to feel contradictory, but stick with it. I have your back.

The first is to talk about what it is that you're manifesting. Talking about what it is that you're creating will absolutely tell you whether you have fully decided that your creation is already yours or not.

If you find yourself:

- Shifting the goal posts: You haven't decided.

- Muttering under your breath as you try to tell people what it is that you're creating: You haven't decided.

- Wanting to change the subject: You haven't decided.

- Diminishing the importance of it: You haven't decided.

You'll know if you still have work to do when it comes to leveling up your identity.

You'll have cracked it when talking about it rolls off your tongue as easily as if you were saying your name, and the feeling in your body is either neutral because it just feels so normal, or excited because the conversation activates you.

This is exactly how I knew that I was going to make £1 million in 2020. It no longer felt weird or embarrassing to own the direction I was going in.

The second thing that may feel contradictory is the fact that you mustn't get lost in thinking that the outcome is the most important thing. You can't think that the outcome is going to make you feel that you are worthwhile. Instead, choose to allow the process of becoming more of who you are, becoming more full of yourself as you 'upgrade' your identity, to be THE thing.

Remember that your evolution is about overflow, because you were born already whole, complete, and enough. So, the invitation is to choose to know more, and own more, of yourself just a little bit (or a lot, if you fancy it) every single day, and to enjoy the process.

Step 4: Enjoy and appreciate

It might be a cliché, but it's a cliché for a reason: It's about the journey, not the destination. You'll spend 90 percent of your time on the journey to being a match for what it is that you desire, and when you get there, your desire isn't going to complete you because, as you already know by now, you're already complete, so the journey has to be what it's about. Focusing on the journey looks like choosing to operate from a place of knowing your greatness, so you're not choosing what you want to prove anything to yourself or others. It looks like allowing yourself to be supported, so that you don't have to walk this path alone. And choosing to be both a generator and conduit for infinite love.

Q: *Have you mastered always operating in your greatness and, if so, I'm curious about the how?*

A: Honestly, no: I haven't. But remember that we don't have to operate in our greatness all the time in order to see massive changes in our lives. My focus is always on seeing how quickly I can notice when the way that I am thinking or behaving is out of alignment with my greatness, and then course-correcting. On a good day, this will happen multiple times, and on a day when I could do better, I will completely forget. I am still a work in progress.

Faith + Action = Miracles

Chapter 12

Pillar of Infinite Conscious Creation - Taking Aligned Action

As we move into the final steps of consciously creating your dream life my hope is that you are feeling more confident and ready than ever. Now is your time.

So far, you have the first four steps down:

1. Identifying what you want

2. Choosing to know that your manifestation is 'already done'

3. Deciding who you need to become

4. Enjoying and appreciating the journey

Before we dive into what's next, I want to highlight what I briefly mentioned in the last chapter about holding the frequency of certainty when it comes to your manifestations. When a person pendulums between knowing that the thing is going to happen, that it's already done, and doubting, they slow down the process of seeing their idea in its physical state. I call this wobbly energy and the more you wobble, the longer it takes.

The reason that this happens is because how you feel impacts the actions you take. If you doubt that the outcome you want is possible, why would you go all in on anything? The underlying thought is, 'This is going to be a waste of my time, energy, and money.' If you doubt that it's possible because you doubt that it's possible for you, then you won't take the aligned action because you will want to avoid looking stupid or embarrassed when it doesn't turn out the way that you want it to. Alternatively, if you have taken the action but second-guessed it every step of the way, your energy is not a match for what it is that you desire.

A friend once told me that one of my superpowers is being able to hold the energy of the transformation until the transformation actually happens – and that is your job. Imagine how you are going to feel once you have manifested what it is that you desire and stay in the feeling for as long as it takes. This is easier for some things than others, but it's necessary for both the small and the big things that you are consciously choosing to create.

I held the intention that my business would make seven figures for about a year and a half. I held that vibration and I was curious to see when I'd be able to tell the story, because I knew it was going to happen. There was a certainty.

One of my previous mentors, Melanie Ann Layer, shared with me a great way to move back into knowing, particularly if all the evidence around you is screaming that you should let it go: Think about how you want to tell the story about who you were on the journey. You'll want to say that you dealt with adversity and non-believers even when you fell flat on your face. Imagine telling the story of your ultimate triumph over adversity every time you are faced with an unexpected challenge, and use the story as a tool to eliminate your lack of certainty.

In my experience, wobbly energy is particularly prevalent when you're close to a breakthrough. You may notice yourself freeze and dissociate from what you want, because you don't trust yourself to hold it. There may be a part of you that doesn't feel safe to fully allow what it is that you are creating, because you are moving into uncharted territory. So, when all of this greatness is just a fingertip away from you, you'll revert to saying, 'I'm too small,' and you'll push it away. That's where the work of the Infinite Greatness, Infinite Support and Infinite Love chapters come into their own.

The inevitability ladder

The first three steps of the manifestation process are like a ladder:

- The first rung is: It is possible.

- The second rung is: It is possible for me.

- And the third rung is: I'm going to take aligned actions to make it happen.

When we pick a goal, we are saying to ourselves that we know that an outcome is possible. But if a person doesn't go through the first three steps of the manifestation process, they don't know that the goal that they have set is actually possible for them. They effectively get stuck on the first rung of the ladder.

In my experience, it helps your journey up the ladder to talk about your goal until it feels like it's already done. Hoping and wishing aren't enough. Or, if they are, they haven't worked for me just yet! What has worked for me is the affirmation that closes every chapter:

Faith + Action = Miracles

Aligned action is a necessary part of the formula. It doesn't necessarily create linear results, i.e. if I do this, then I can guarantee that that will happen. The energetics of conscious creation and manifestation don't work like that. Oftentimes, you will be taking action that feels aligned and it will look like nothing is happening at all. This isn't easy unless you make the process, and who you're becoming on the journey, the main aim of the game. When you do this, you make it far easier for you to take aligned action in the direction of what it is that you desire.

For example, your goal is to bring in more clients this month than last month. So, you make the intention to enjoy the process of selling over the phone more than you have ever done before. You don't go in to every call wondering if this person is going to be the person that says yes, you go in wondering how you can enjoy this call more than the last one. Focusing on the process rather than the outcome will revolutionize how you approach every single goal that you set for yourself and make the conscious manifestation process way easier to stick with because you have already decided that the goal is possible for you. Although you're not in control of when the manifestation will present itself, you know that the more you focus on optimizing who you are being in the process of it manifesting, the quicker it will show up.

Frequently, you'll be doing the work with your right hand, and that'll be where you expect the results, but the manifestation will actually show up in your left hand. Some people think that this means that the manifestation sequence hasn't worked for them, but that isn't true. The manifestation shows up however it wants to show up; it's beyond your control.

You see, when we take aligned action and combine it with that feeling of certainty, knowing, and appreciation that we are the creator of all things, the energy builds and encircles us, creating a magnetic field that pulls the manifestation into our being. We have to keep an open mind about how and when it will show up, and avoid negating it if it arrives in an unexpected way.

Taking aligned action

To move on to the third rung of the inevitability ladder, you need to move from possibility to probability, from possible to possible for me, to probable for me. You're probably not going to like the next step from there. To be honest, even I don't like it! But we've got this far and I've actually been talking about this under various different guises since the beginning of the book. So, what is it? Consistency. Taking aligned action consistently over time is what will move you into WHO you need to become to be a match for what it is that you desire. You'll turn possible to possible for me, to probable and, finally, inevitable.

I invite you to remember that inevitable doesn't have a timeline, or at least it isn't working to yours. In my experience, as a person uplevels their identity and expands even more into their own unique and limitless potential, the quicker the manifestations show up. But that isn't really even the point anymore is it? The point is being able to enjoy who you're becoming as you create more miracles.

> *Our purpose and our mission is to*
> *become more of ourselves.*

Now, I'm going to share with you a few techniques that will help you to take aligned action. They may or may not be useful to you, and they're certainly not needed or mandatory, but they have worked for me.

Visualization

If you are a visual person and you like to be able to see what it is that you're creating, then creating a visual representation of your desires, and remembering to tune in to how it's going to FEEL when you are living your manifestation, could be a super-useful tool for you.

I love to use creative visualization in my mind's eye. Athletes have used this powerful technique for years, picturing themselves running around the track, crossing the finish line, holding up a cup. This consistent visualization, and the feelings that go along with it, create new neural pathways in the mind. Our subconscious actively looks for experiences and situations that will replicate or lead us toward the end vision, because of the positive association we have created with it through our elevated emotions.

Do you need to do it daily for it to work? Will it accelerate the speed at which you create the necessary neural pathways? The science says, absolutely. Repetition of any action, real or imagined, creates new memories for the brain to operate from. The aim of the game is to remember as frequently as possible who it is that we are becoming and what it is that we are creating, because it's so easy to forget. This is why Joe Dispenza says that he doesn't get up from his creative visualization until he has become a new person, until he has become 'that' person, so he can't forget.

Meditation

Meditation can be really useful in helping you to reset your state of being. Silent meditation can help you to create your own visualizations, while guided meditation can be good if you find it useful to have another person's words guiding you toward certain feelings or emotions.

I particularly love meditations that guide me into speaking with my 'highest self' and healing the parts of myself that don't feel safe to progress on the journey toward my manifestation, the parts of myself that cause me to procrastinate or self-sabotage.

Affirmations and intention setting

If the mind remembers everything, is it necessary for you to write out what it is that you want 500 times a day like some manifestation techniques suggest? No, it's not necessary in order to manifest what you want, but the act of writing your desire down can be a helpful reminder that you are choosing to show up and take action in alignment with your goals.

Generally, I have found affirmations incredibly helpful in expanding and upgrading my whole way of thinking. Some of my favorite ones include:

- 'Faith + Action = Miracles.' (Obviously, that one has changed my entire life.)

- 'Everything is always working out for me. The smallest actions lead to the biggest results because I'm just lucky like that.'

- 'I am whole, complete, and enough.'

- 'I am worthy and deserving.'

- 'I am getting better and better at [insert thing] every day.'

- 'I am so lovable.'

- 'I love my life.'

- 'I wake up feeling happy and excited.'

Affirmations work by programming your subconscious. However, they can work against you if you find yourself arguing for a reality that is yet to reflect what you are saying to yourself. So, a super-simple way to neutralize any internal conflict is to simply add the words:

Every day, I am becoming more _____.

That *absolutely* gets to be your truth as you take aligned action toward the intention.

Journaling

We have used journaling quite a lot so far in this book, but let me tell you about another one of my favorite ways to use this tool, which is to write out the journey to my manifestation in past tense: How I got there, how I felt during key moments of the journey, and how I managed the ups and downs.

You can also record this as a voice note that you can listen to daily. Create a five- to ten-minute recording where you talk about your journey in the past tense, and then listen to yourself celebrating your journey with feeling and emotion.

A Future You party

If you have a group of friends who are reading this book with you, or simply understand what you are choosing to create for your life, why not throw a Future You party? It's an incredible opportunity to get dressed up as your future self and then speak as though you have already achieved what it is that you desire ALL night long. It's not always easy to stay in character, but it's so fun. And, just like with everything else, when you notice yourself slipping, all you have to do is choose to lean back in.

Remembering to remember

One of the greatest gifts that you can give to yourself is remembering that when you try and work out all of the exact steps to HOW you are going to achieve something, you slow down the pace of your manifestation. Your tunnel vision makes it difficult to notice all of the signs, serendipitous opportunities, and wild coincidences that will inevitably present themselves to you on the journey to you becoming who you were always meant to be.

If someone had said to me 10 years ago that the path to getting not my first, but my second, book deal would be like this, I would have said, 'don't be ridiculous.' I couldn't have worked this out with the best crystal ball in the world. And yet, in these pages, I'm sharing with you the lessons that started presenting themselves to me through various books, mentors, teachers, and my own discoveries not just over the last decade, but over the course of my life. So, hold your plans loosely, focus on the next best step and WHO you need to become to be a match for what it is that your soul desires, and choose to know that when the time is right, the Universe will wow you a million times over, because this is the path of the Infinite Receiver.

Taking the next step

To be super clear, whilst all of the techniques that I have listed above will help you get closer to what you desire, they will only work if you actually take aligned action. For example, whilst it's true that someone might just walk in off the street and make you an offer on your house, you'll increase your chances of selling it if you have a 'for sale' board outside, so you need to go to a real estate agent and put your house on the market. If you want to start a business, your first aligned action should be deciding on what it is that you want to do, then telling your friends and family about it, and designing your first product and package. You don't need to know every single step before you get started, but you do need to take the next step and do something. And what's even cooler is that it doesn't even have to be the 'right' next step. It just needs to be a step, because that step will tell you whether you're on the right track or if you need to pivot. And it's absolutely fine if you find that you need to pivot 100 times before you know that you're on the right track. That's just the nature of business. You don't need to get it right all the time, but you do need to move.

To recap, your 5 steps to consciously co-creating your dream life are:

1. Identifying what you want

2. Choosing to know that your manifestation is already done

3. Deciding who you need to become

4. Enjoying and appreciating the journey

5. Taking aligned action

So, let's get going!

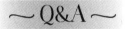

~ Q&A ~

Q: How do I accept myself needing to learn more before I can manifest what I desire?

A: When you switch your focus from the end result to who you are becoming on the journey to receiving and being aligned with the result, and take the necessary aligned action, you will become a match for what you're manifesting so much faster. You'll also get to notice all of the magic that you will inevitably create on your way to 'the thing.'

If that feels like something to be disappointed about, you get to ask yourself, why? What are you making the manifestation mean? Because if it means that you'll be good enough, or better in any way, you know that you need to go back and dive deeper into the first three Pillars.

If it's because you feel that you 'need' the manifestation now, focus on the Pillar of Infinite Support. Then, you'll remember that you will always be supported as you continue to take action toward the bigger vision you have for yourself. You'll know that everything is always working out for you. And the more that you are able to take action from this place of certainty, rather than lack, the more you are creating a solid energetic foundation for you to amplify your conscious receiving – and that is so exciting.

Faith + Action = Miracles

Final Thoughts

Can you believe it? We've reached the end of our journey through the pages of this book! But this isn't where the story ends. One thing I say in my programs, and the way I approach this work in my own life, is that it's ongoing. There's always room for deepening. Whenever you want to open yourself up to receiving more, you get to reconnect with the Pillars and go deeper. Ask yourself the questions that you have found in the pages of this book and new ones of your own that relate to who you are becoming, and where you're going next, as opposed to where you have been.

It's an ongoing journey that will never be about creating the perfect life. It's not a case of, 'If I follow the Infinite Receiving process and I get it all right, everything is going to be perfect for me.' It's about you being able to be in the dance of life, understanding your limitless power and potency. And, as you do that, you're going to be able to navigate the inevitable challenges that arise from a place of deep connection with yourself as you approach your life from a place of knowing that you're whole, complete, and enough. That right there is the prize of the game that we are all playing. And when we live from that place, everything we create externally can be created with way less stress and much more ease, as we realize that it's simply a beautiful bonus.

On the days when you're feeling off, it's about remembering to see, so ask yourself: 'How quickly can I remember who I am? How quickly can I remember why I'm doing what I'm doing? How quickly can I remember my potency? How quickly can I remember that I'm a divine and unique expression of the original Source of all things? How quickly can I remember my limitlessness?' That is the game of life from now on.

It only requires one degree a day, as small steps every single day will change your entire life. By activating the Four Pillars of Infinite Receiving – Infinite Greatness, Infinite Support, Infinite Love, and Infinite Conscious Creation – you'll recognize that every opportunity, every moment in life, you are receiving. And receiving infinitely. And the fairy dust on top, so to speak, is that the more you bring your conscious awareness back to knowing your limitless capacity, the easier it becomes for you to create and receive what it is that you desire. From a place of fullness, feeling safe and powerful, and not just seeing the magic but being the magic, is effortless.

I invite you to dip back into the book frequently, particularly when you feel ready for more expansion in your life or you are having a wobble. Re-read the whole thing or use this book like an oracle deck by opening whichever page calls to you to prompt you into remembering again.

I'm grateful for the process of writing this book because it's been an excellent mirror for me. It's shown me where I really am in the work myself, and it's shown me all the places where I forget my greatness, which has been simultaneously humbling and empowering. I got to see where I can offer myself more compassion and where the opportunity is for further expansion. This is the dance. It's not about getting to the final destination, it's about who I am choosing to be now, and I am truly grateful to recognize that this is the journey.

I hope that you, too, feel inspired by these pages. I hope that you realize just how much you already have access to and that you feel excited by the potential and the possibility that's there for you. It's also my hope that you already know that you are a walking miracle; you are special just as you are right now.

Most of all, I hope that you realize the impact that you, as a conscious, wealthy entrepreneur, can have – the ripple effect, the tidal wave, the positive impact that can be created when you have your inner and outer world aligned.

Together, we can ignite a whole new level of receiving that comes from a place of wholeness. When you know your greatness, know you are infinitely supported, and know you are a portal for infinite love, then, alongside being able to consciously create whatever it is that you desire, I genuinely believe that we can change the entire planet. We get to be the model for that change. There's a real opportunity to transform the fabric of the world through Infinite Receiving – and that is my mission. And as you join me on this magical adventure, I hope that one day soon it will be yours, too.

Faith + Action = Miracles

Resources

Websites

- My website: www.suzyashworth.com
- Infinite Receiving Portal: www.infinitereceivingbook.com
- Infinite Receiving Online Community: @infinitereceiving
- The Wheel of Infinite Receiving:
  www.suzyashworth.com/infinitereceivingwheel
- My 2019 prediction: www.infinitereceivingbook.com/prediction
- One-degree-a-day reminders:
  www.suzyashworth.com/onedegreeaday

Podcast

- *Infinite Receiving* is available on Apple Podcasts and Spotify.

Music playlist

- www.suzyashworth.com/infinitereceivingplaylist

Acknowledgments

I want to thank Doreen and Dennis Poccock, my beloved foster parents. Their legacy of devotion lives on through me daily, and my relationship with them continues to grow as I continue to grow and evolve. I am so deeply grateful for the lessons that continue to unfold in my life.

I am deeply grateful to Flora and Sunny Atavwigho – without your union there would be no me. I have learned so much about faith from you especially, Mum, and what it means for that to be unwavering. Thank you.

Thank you to my sister Tara Humphrey for choosing me. I love you so deeply. I am so deeply grateful for your support and your belief in me, and your ability to believe in me sometimes more than I believe in myself. Thank you.

Thank you to Sarah Jane Rawlins. You changed my life when you came into it over 25 years ago and shared the book *The* Celestine Prophecy with me. That share changed my field of vision and awareness, and I began to be able to put words to things I had observed happening that I couldn't quite articulate. Your love for life, your enormous heart, and your support of me is something that I can never take for granted.

Kyle Gray, thank you for the hand you had in helping to bring this book to life. Thank you for being a trailblazer and proof that you get to do it your way. I love you and appreciate your support deeply. Thank you.

Thank you to my dear mentors both near and far: Regan Hillyer and JuanPa Barahona, Melanie Ann Layer, Niyc Pidgeon, Layla Martin, and everyone else who helped me crack open my heart in the writing of this book.

Thank you to #TeamSuzy and your unwavering support during the writing of this book; I love you so much.

Thank you to all of the clients who have run with me over the last decade; you have directly and indirectly helped to co-create this book with me. I love you so much. Thank you.

Thank you to Jerome Ashworth. Who we are together in this chapter means more to me than you will ever know.

Victoria Adamson

About the Author

Suzy Ashworth is a single mum of three children, high school dropout, Hay House author, international keynote speaker, multiple seven-figure success coach, and serial entrepreneur on a mission. Over the last ten years, she has worked with thousands of impact-driven leaders in business to create quantum shifts in their lives and their businesses. Her vision is to raise the vibration of humanity by helping people to consciously create freedom, joy, and abundance and sharing the secrets of how to tap into the frequency of Infinite Receiving. Her work has been featured in *Forbes, Grazia,* and the BBC.

 suzyashworth.com

f **SuzyAshworth2**

 suzy_ashworth

 @LimitlessyouCoUk